Preaching in Pictures

Other Books in The Artistry of Preaching Series

Preaching as Poetry: Beauty, Goodness, and Truth in Every Sermon
by Paul Scott Wilson

Actuality: Real Life Stories for Sermons That Matter
by Scott Hoezee

The Artistry of Preaching Series

Preaching in Pictures

Using Images for
Sermons That Connect

Peter Jonker

 Abingdon Press
Nashville

PREACHING IN PICTURES:
USING IMAGES FOR SERMONS THAT CONNECT

Copyright © 2015 by Abingdon Press

Library of Congress Cataloging-in-Publication Data

Jonker, Peter (Peter M.)
    Preaching in pictures : using images for sermons that connect / Peter Jonker.
        pages cm. — (The artistry of preaching series)
    Includes bibliographical references.
    ISBN 978-1-4267-8192-6 (binding)
    1. Preaching. 2. Image (Theology) 3. Homiletical illustrations. I. Title.
    BV4226.J66 2015
    251'.08—dc23

                                                                                2015000524

15 16 17 18 19 20 21 22 23 24—10 9 8 7 6 5 4 3 2 1
MANUFACTURED IN THE UNITED STATES OF AMERICA

True ease in writing comes from art, not chance,
As those move easiest who have learn'd to dance.
Alexander Pope, "An Essay on Criticism"

If you want to build a ship, don't drum up people together to collect
wood and don't assign them tasks and work, but rather teach them to
long for the endless immensity of the sea.
Antoine de Saint-Exupéry

Contents

Series Preface

The Artistry of Preaching series gives practical guidance on matters that receive insufficient attention in preaching literature yet that are key for preachers seeking greater creativity in their preaching. Fresh, faithful proclamation requires imagination and creative engagement of the Bible and our world. There is no shortage of commentaries on the Bible and books on biblical interpretation for preaching, but the practical resources to help strengthen the creativity of preachers to help them better to proclaim the gospel are much in need.

The first volume of this series, *Preaching as Poetry: Beauty, Goodness, and Truth in Every Sermon*, redefines preaching for our current postmodern age. Imagination is needed to compose strong theological sermons. Modernist notions of authority, goodness, and truth are challenged by our current culture. The church needs to adapt to a new world, where faith is understood as poetry rooted in the beauty, goodness, and truth of a saving relationship with God.

The second volume of this series, *Actuality: Real Life Stories for Sermons That Matter*, is a resource for preachers who want guidance to be better storytellers or to use story more effectively to communicate with a new generation. There readers will also find a collection of stories that both preach and that can stimulate their own imaginations to identify stories from their own contexts. Preachers can easily run out of good stories to use that embody the gospel. The problem is not a shortage of stories—they are all around in everyday events; the task is learning how to harvest them, as is shown in this volume. Preachers long for good stories, and today's listeners are not content with the canned Internet illustrations that sound artificial and have a predictable moral. Rather they want stories rooted in the actual world in which they live, that depict life as they know it, and that can function as Jesus's stories did, as parables and metaphors that bear God's grace to their hearers.

This third volume of The Artistry of Preaching series, *Preaching in Pictures: Using Images for Sermons That Connect* by Peter Jonker, helps preachers add some spark and imagination to their preaching of the sort that can be provided by effective use of a dominant or controlling image. The challenge is not just to find images that are visually captivating or evocative; it is to find ones that are artistic, "propulsive," and theologically centered, helping the sermon to communicate God's saving grace. By moving from a theme sentence to a goal to a controlling image statement, preachers can move their composition from being a "beautiful mess" to an effective and affective sermon with creative power. Preachers will be engaged by practical exercises adapted from creative writers and poets that help in the art of selecting images and polishing them for use in relation to biblical texts. Equally important in these current times, readers will find guidance on using images on screens in worship as controlling images for sermons. The word comes first, and developing the craft of preaching can powerfully assist the work of the Spirit and increase the joy of preaching.

The aim of the series is to be practical, to provide concrete guidelines and exercises for preachers to follow, to assist them in engaging practice. Preaching is much more than art, yet by ensuring that we as preachers employ artistry in our preaching, we assist the Holy Spirit in communicating the gospel to a new generation of people seeking God.

—Paul Scott Wilson, Series Editor

Acknowledgments

I've spent more than twenty-five years thinking about sermons, and there have been many companions along the path: teachers, listeners, encouragers, critics, supporters, conversation partners. I couldn't possibly acknowledge all the people who have walked beside me on the path and helped me sort out the craft of preaching. But I'll try.

Thank you to the congregations of Woodlawn Christian Reformed Church and LaGrave Avenue Christian Reformed Church. I served Woodlawn for twenty years, starting from the day I toddled out of seminary and continuing all the way into the relatively confident steps of middle age. The people of Woodlawn put up with my early sermonic mistakes, stood by me in all my insecurities. They gave me room to grow and sustained me with encouragement along the way. I am forever grateful to them. They are my friends. More recently I've started down the path as pastor at LaGrave, and I have received the same patience and the same grace. LaGrave blessed me with the unprecedented gift of a summer sabbatical after only eight months service. Without that time, this book wouldn't exist. I thank God for LaGrave and Woodlawn.

I would also like to thank some of my colleagues. Here, too, the list is long: John Timmer, who first suggested that I should see Bible texts like paintings; Mike Abma, with whom I joyfully shared a pulpit for fifteen years; Neal Plantinga, whose sermons first woke me up to the craft of preaching; Scott Hoezee, my friend at Calvin Seminary who encouraged me through the writing process; and John Rottman, another seminary colleague who first made me believe that these ideas were worth a book and who gently pushed me down the path toward completion.

Paul Scott Wilson's experience has been invaluable in this process. He read the manuscript multiple times and helped this first-time writer understand what worked in a book and what didn't. Paul, thank you for your patience and your thoroughness. Thanks also to Connie Stella, Kelsey Spinnato, and the other members of the Abingdon editorial staff. You put up with the naiveté of a first-time writer who knew nothing of the labyrinthine intricacies of copyright and fair use.

I want to thank my parents. My dad gets credit for reading the manuscript and helpfully commenting, but Mom and Dad's true contribution to this book was more seminal. God used my parents to plant in me the idea that sermons mattered. When I was a child, they took me to church every Sunday, they listened to sermons with hungry attention, and they lived out of the word they heard preached.

But most of all I want to thank my wife and my children. Linda, Katherine, Patrick, and Abby, you have given up twenty-two years of weekends so that I could follow this call. Not only that, you are the ones who endured the anxieties and frustrations that didn't show on the pulpit or in the fellowship hall. Thank you for putting up with all my self-flagellation and obsessive polishing. Of course you did more than put up with me; every day you surrounded me with laughter, affection, companionship, and joy.

The Controlling Image

Taming the Beautiful Mess

S ermons start with a beautiful mess.

After fifteen years of writing sermons every week, I saw that my sermon preparation followed a predictable pattern. If you're a preacher, see if this resonates with you. If you're not, welcome to my world! An average week of sermon preparation looks something like this: You start with a biblical text; maybe it's one that you chose that week, maybe it's one that's been assigned as part of a sermon series, maybe it's out of the lectionary. It doesn't matter. On Tuesday morning (or maybe Monday) you open your Bible and start your sermonic journey. You read the passage carefully and prayerfully. As you read you ask yourself, *What is God saying to me here? What is God saying to our congregation?* Inevitably this careful reading leads to various thoughts and observations. You write these down. Sometimes the passage reminds you of a story you heard, or something that C. S. Lewis once said, or maybe it reminds you of a poem. You jot down these things too.

After reading it in English, you dig into the Greek (or Hebrew) version of your text. What are the passage's key words? Does the English capture the full sense of the Greek? Are there other nuances in the original language that the English versions can't translate? If your level of proficiency in the biblical languages is similar to mine, this can be a painstaking process. But it's necessary, so you do the digging, and anything your language study unearths gets thrown onto the pile.

Next come commentaries. Devout scholars have thought about your Bible passage for two thousand years, creating a treasure trove of communal insight. You have to spend at least some time at their feet. Between your bookshelf commentaries and the online materials, you have a mountain of information on your text right at your fingertips. You plow through as much as you can and make notes on all the exegetical issues you find. There are usually a couple dozen issues per text, which means you scribble several pages of notes detailing the various interpretive debates and questions. You throw these notes into the exegetical mix.

On top of what the commentaries say, there are also topical books of theology and spirituality that apply to your text. Suppose, for example, you're preaching on the Holy Spirit. It's a good idea to poke your head into a book or two to see what the great theologians of the past have said about the Spirit's work. So you read a couple of pages of Calvin; you take a look at your favorite contemporary book of systematic theology; you do due theological diligence. Again, whenever you read something interesting, something illuminating, you put it on the pile.

When all these investigations are over, by Thursday morning you have what might be best described as a beautiful mess. You have dozens of stories, assorted insights, scribbled Greek words, pages of quotes, stacks of observations, note cards with little insights hand-scrawled on them, books stacked upside down and opened to a favorite passage—the treasures of your exegetical digging scattered across your desk. Much of this material is exciting. The Spirit and the Word have given you quite a treasure mound. The passage has moved and challenged you; it has opened your eyes. It really is beautiful stuff you've found! But it's a mess.

And this beautiful mess presents you with what is in my experience the main problem of preaching: Somehow you have to take this beautiful mess and shape it into an orderly sermon (mine tend to be twenty minutes). You have to take this chaos of exciting observations and craft a disciplined message that speaks to everyone in the congregation: young and old, rich and poor, the joyful and the distressed, the skeptics and the deeply believing. *And* you have to speak to these people in all their dimensions. Your sermon must touch the listeners in their hearts as well as their minds.

Here is where preaching becomes very, very, very hard. How do you find your way through the beautiful mess? Where do you begin your journey? What treasures do you pull out of the pile to show to the people? Which insights do you leave for another time? How do you organize this material into a coherent, artistic whole?

Artistic is just the right word here. Moving from the beautiful mess to a finished sermon is an artistic task. The ability to take the information gathered from hard exegesis and make it into a winning sermon is a creative endeavor that rivals the craft of any painter, musician, or poet.

In my experience, seminary prepared me very well for making the beautiful mess. I was equipped with the exegetical, linguistic, historical, and theological tools to gather all sorts of treasures from a single biblical text. In the words of one of my classmates, seminary made me into an "exegetical ninja." But when it came to taking my beautiful mess and making it into an effective and affective sermon, I was mostly left to my own devices. I moved ahead but worked mainly by intuition and feel.

To put this in Fred Craddock's terms, I left seminary feeling equipped for the hard-chair side of sermon preparation but not for the soft-chair side.[1] Craddock tells students that good preachers need two chairs to finish their sermons. The preacher starts by sitting in the hard chair. That's where you do your rigorous exegetical work: the language study, the commentary reading, the theological reflection. It's a hard chair because this material is gathered only by disciplined work and intense study. This is the chair in which you accumulate the beautiful mess.

The second chair is the soft chair of creative reflection. This chair is more comfortable, a living room armchair instead of an upright desk chair, the sort of chair in which you can lean back and let your imagination wander. Here is where you dream up connections and stories and analogies. Here is where you begin to craft. Here is where you begin to shape your beautiful mess into a meaningful sermon. I feel like seminary gave me lots of tools for the hard-chair side of sermon making but relatively few for my time in the soft chair.

This book will provide some tools for the soft chair. It won't provide *all* of them. Writing a sermon is an extraordinarily complex task and there are hundreds of books to be written on how to make a sermon out of the beautiful mess. Read a broader study of homiletics, like Paul Wilson's wonderful book, *The Four Pages of the Sermon*[2] or Thomas G. Long's *The Witness of Preaching*,[3] and you get a sense of the complexity. I will not reflect on all the parts of sermon preparation, and I do not suggest that the observations I offer are sufficient for creating great sermons. The homiletical toolbox needs to be stocked with many tools; I'm reflecting on only one of them, and it's critically important. For the preacher looking to make that step from the beautiful mess to an ordered, meaningful sermon, I think it's one of the best tools available. I'm thinking of the controlling image. Learning to use controlling images effectively is central to the craft of preaching.

3

What is a controlling image? I will explain it more fully later, but for now let me offer this definition: a controlling image is an evocative picture or scene that shows up repeatedly in a sermon and communicates either the trouble or the grace of the sermon theme, therefore helping to accomplish the sermon's goal.

In Defense of Sermon Craft

Before we look at what it takes to shape a controlling image and before we get too deep into the art of shaping an image, let me say a few words about the place of craft in sermon making.

I minister in the Reformed tradition, which places a strong emphasis on the sovereignty of God. In my tradition the Spirit leads the work of salvation and all human action is a grateful response to the Spirit's work. As a result, when preachers talk too much about the craft of preaching and the art of sermon making, some people begin to worry. Are we paying too much attention to artifice? Are we studying how to manipulate people with our rhetoric? Is homiletics becoming a specialized form of marketing? Are we, by all our human craft, edging the Holy Spirit out of the picture?

This is a real concern. Every time a task requires human skill, every time we do a job that requires our intellect and our effort, we run the risk of moving the spotlight from our Lord to ourselves. Anytime we do work that others might admire and praise for its excellence, we are at some level of spiritual risk.

How do you handle that risk?

You could simply avoid applying human skill and excellence. You could avoid any kind of work where others might praise you, and where you might be tempted toward pride. You could simply bury your gift. But surely that's not what God intends. At least one of the lessons learned in the parable of the talents (Matt 25:14-30) is that God wants us to use our gifts and skills so that the kingdom might be built. In this parable, the servant who chooses not to use his talent doesn't fare so well.

The other option is to strive to use every gift to the best of your ability, to take every talent and develop it to its fullest extent, but to do it with humility so that everything is done for the glory of God. That seems the more biblical route. That sounds like Paul in 1 Corinthians 10:31: "So, whether you eat or drink or whatever you do, you should do it all for God's glory."[4]

In my tradition, people have been comfortable when preachers exercise the gift of the intellect in the work of exegesis, using the excellence of their minds to make theological distinctions and translate verbs and appeal to the listener's reason; we have been less comfortable when the creative gifts are used to create beauty and appeal to the imagination. This is an unfair bias. Both faculties are gifts of God. Both faculties can be used in the building of the kingdom. Both faculties can be abused and manipulated for personal gain. Both faculties are meant to be used in humility, under the direction of the Holy Spirit, for the glory of God.[5]

Besides, as Paul Scott Wilson clearly recognizes, it's impossible to preach a sermon without *some* sort of craft:

> Typically preachers add something to the biblical text. To tell a biblical tale effectively one does not simply repeat it. One puts the text—whether a story from the gospels or a passage from the epistles—into one's own words and adds emphasis and emotion. One retells it in a life-like setting, usually as an episode in some faith journey. One adds certain pieces of information to it to make it come to life in the present day, and this can leave the preacher open to the charge of distorting or otherwise misrepresenting the text. Every time we preach a biblical text, no matter what method we use—classical exposition or contemporary narrative—we add something to the text that is not in it, be it history, geography, archaeology, translation, tradition, explicit discussion of a doctrine, information from other texts, or understanding and experiences from our own settings and cultures. It is impossible to preach by keeping the biblical text in the sermon exactly as it is in the Bible.[6]

We are not Docetists. We believe in the Word made flesh who walked among us, we believe that at Pentecost the Spirit filled the church, body and soul, and we have seen that the very first movement of that Spirit caused Peter to preach a sermon, a sermon rich in craft that didn't just speak to people's minds; it cut them to the heart.

The Sermon Theme and Its (Limited) Uses

When it comes to taming the beautiful mess, homileticians have done a good deal of thinking. Significant ink has been spilled telling preachers how to turn their pile of exegetical notes into a sermon. Usually that advice starts with the sermon theme.

Discussions of sermon theme are everywhere in homiletics books. Virtually all these books insist that preachers center their sermons on a theme sentence. There's a good reason why beginning preachers hear their instructors insist on a sermon theme, why most of us practicing preachers usually spend a little time every week trying to write down the subject of our sermon in one pithy sentence: bad sermons lack focus and limp in seven different directions, leaving the listeners unable to articulate what they just heard. So, for generations, homiletic orthodoxy has been: sermons must be about one thing!

"Proper theme formulation is intended to keep the sermon on the right track," says Sid Greidanus, and he quotes homiletician Donald Miller to reinforce his point: "Any sermon worthy of the name should have a theme. . . . Ideally any single sermon should have just one major idea . . . two or three or four points which are not part of the same great idea do not make a sermon—they are two, three or four sermons all preached on one occasion."[7] Bryan Chappell shares this perspective: "Sermons of any significant length contain theological concepts, illustrative materials and corroborative facts. These components, however, do not imply that a sermon is about many things. Each feature of a well-wrought message reflects, refines, and/ or develops one major idea."[8] In The *Witness of Preaching*, instead of using the language of theme, Tom Long talks about a focus statement, "a concise statement of the central, controlling and unifying theme of the sermon," and he thinks every sermon should have one.[9] While some recent homileticians have raised questions about themes, calling them rationalistic and reductionistic (Eugene Lowry is one of these questioners), most teachers of preaching agree that every sermon needs a central focus, a main idea, a unifying statement, a theme. In the first volume of this present series, Paul Scott Wilson has compared the theme sentence in the sermon to the focal point in a work of art and says it is "the single most important source of unity and hence beauty in a sermon."[10]

A good theme has many uses. When it is properly derived from the text, it provides a focal point that keeps the preacher from wandering off into extrabiblical speculation. When openly stated in the body of the sermon, it helps the listener follow. Ultimately, however, a theme often can't get the preacher very far down the sermon-writing road. This is because it's too simple, too narrow a statement to really inspire. Listen to some of the themes suggested by homileticians in their preaching books and you'll see what I mean. Sid Greidanus suggests that the sermon theme[11] for John 13:12-17 should be "Followers of Christ ought to render humble service to one another"; the theme of Jeremiah 9:23-24 could be "Glory in knowing the Lord"; and for 1 Timothy 4:7-8 it could be, "Train yourself in godliness."[12] These are good themes as far as they go. They are clearly based on the text and they provide a focal point, but if the preacher writes this theme at the top of his or her sermon manuscript on Thursday morning as he or she prepares to write, does he or she feel inspired by this theme? Does the preacher feel ready to put pen to paper? Does the preacher have a clear idea about how to make this sermon sing? I doubt it. Most preachers I know need a lot more than "train yourself in godliness" before they are ready to start writing. A bare proposition is simply not enough to anchor a sermon—it's merely a good start.

Of course not all homileticians suggest theme sentences that are quite so spare. Tom Long admits that for a pastor preaching on John 5:1-18—the story of the healing at the pool of Bethesda—a theme such as "Jesus was a controversial healer" is "too broad to be genuinely helpful to the preacher." Long promotes lengthier, more detailed thematic constructions, ones that give the preacher a little more clay to knead. So, for a sermon on Romans 8:28-39 Long suggests the theme: "Because we have seen in Jesus Christ that God is for us, we can be confident that God loves us and cares for us even when our experience seems to deny it."[13] That's definitely an improvement. The preacher has more to work with.

Paul Scott Wilson also holds out for richer themes, although his concern isn't so much length as vibrancy. He wants preachers to write themes that use God-active language.[14] He says theme sentences need to proclaim the action of a living God in our lives. Theme sentences like "God wants Israel to change" or "Jesus calls us to repent" are too weak. They make people the main actors in the drama of salvation. Better that the theme have God as the subject of a vivid, active verb. So instead of "God wants Israel to change," Wilson suggests "God brings Israel to a new place," and instead of "Jesus calls us to repent," Wilson suggests "Jesus brings us to repentance."[15] For preachers trying to cook up higher-octane themes, Wilson offers five rules for theme construction:

1. Keep it short.

2. Make it a declarative sentence (not a question).

3. Make God the subject of the sentence.

4. Focus on God's action of grace.

5. Use strong, active verbs.[16]

I like almost everything Wilson says about themes here. Themes that follow his five rules will indeed lead to better sermons. Nevertheless, a theme sentence like "Jesus brings us to repentance" still doesn't do very much to stimulate our imaginations. It may keep a sermon from going off the road, it may keep a sermon from getting lost in the woods of asides and distractions, it may keep the focus on God's action, but it can't in itself propel us down the road toward a really strong, imaginative sermon that touches the heart and the head. A theme is a nice, basic, rational statement of the message's center, but there's not much here to inspire or move.

Adding a Goal Statement

Recognizing that even the best themes are a little homiletically thin, people who write about preaching have tried to fatten them up with the addition of sermon goals. Before a preacher starts writing, they say, he or she ought to have a good sermon theme *and* a good sermon goal.[17] Fred Craddock and the homileticians of his generation saw that sermons based on a theme alone were deficient. A theme may be a faithful communication of what a biblical text says, but a biblical text doesn't just say something, it also does something. It is a living witness. A biblical text doesn't just speak the rational language of a theme, a biblical text also hits you; it has impact at all levels of human perception, not just reason.

As the preacher does his or her exegesis in the study, the preacher isn't simply informed and educated by the text; he or she is *moved* by the text, challenged, delighted, frightened, confused, embraced by the text. The preacher's mind is stimulated. The preacher's heart is warmed. A beautiful vision fills the preacher's head. But then he or she forms the theme and that rich experience is reduced to a proposition. That proposition becomes the seed the preacher plants in the ground and tries to grow into a sermon. But what kind of tree will grow from this propositional seed? The sermon that sprouts from that proposition will be a mostly rational plant, bearing propositional fruit. Much of the delight, the warmth, and the beauty will be lost. To quote Tom Long, "The joy of 'Eureka!' becomes, in the sermon, the dull thud of 'My thesis for this morning is . . .'"[18]

> No one who reads a rousing novel or sees a powerful play or views a provocative movie would be tempted to squeeze those rich experiences into only one "main idea." Engaging a biblical text is at least as multifaceted as any of those encounters, and while ideas are surely uncovered in biblical interpretation, there are also moods, movements, conflicts, epiphanies, and other experiences that cannot be pressed into a strictly ideational mold.[19]

Recognizing the truth of these sorts of observations, modern homileticians have struggled to find ways to express not only what a text means, but also what it *does*. As part of the struggle they've called on preachers to formulate sermon goals as well as sermon themes. A sermon theme will express what you want your sermon to say. A purpose or goal statement will say what you want your sermon to do. Greidanus explains the distinction this way:

> When the Old Testament prophets confronted the wayward people of God, when they announced impending destruction because of continued disobedience, the theme of the text would be something like: "The Lord will destroy his people." For a passage like Jeremiah 4, this represents *what* the text is saying. The goal or purpose of the text is related to the theme, but it tells what the prophet is trying to do when he preaches. So for Jeremiah 4 the prophet is trying to accomplish "Israel's repentance and salvation."[20]

Tom Long makes the same point, but he doesn't use theme and goal language; he speaks instead of focus and function: "What the sermon aims to say can be called its 'focus,' and what the sermon aims to do can be called its 'function.'" Whereas a focus statement describes what the sermon is *about*, "A *function statement* is a description of what the preacher hopes the sermon will create or *cause to happen* for the hearers."[21] As was the case with his focus (theme) statements, Long's function statements are more elaborate than Greidanus's (helpfully so). So for Romans 8:28-39, Long offers the focus statement: "Because we have seen in Jesus Christ that God is *for* us, we can be confident that God loves and cares for us even when our experience seems to deny it." The accompanying function statement, the statement he uses to identify "what the preacher hopes the sermon will create or cause to happen" is "to reassure and give hope to troubled hearers in the midst of, not apart from, their distress."[22]

The addition of a purpose statement to the theme is an improvement. It certainly recognizes that sermons need to aim at more than the intellect. But I know from experience that having a nicely formatted theme and goal at the top of your page is still not enough to help your sermon move. I may have identified what I want my sermon to "cause to happen" in my hearers, but I haven't done anything to figure out how to make that happen. I have my goal/function statement for Romans 8:28-39 neatly typed in front of me, and I know what I want to do, but how on earth am I going to "reassure and give hope to troubled hearers in the midst of, not apart from, their distress"? This is the hard part of preaching. I know I want my congregation to hope, I know I want my congregation to be reassured, but how do I spark hope and reassurance? Disciplined study and a little clear thinking have brought me to the point where I can name the emotional spiritual results I'm seeking for the congregation, but the hard part of preaching, the really difficult aspect, is to help my listeners to know—in the deep place where intellect and feeling and commitment come together—the reassurance of the living God.

Because it's so hard to create this spark in your hearers, and because preachers don't always feel that they have the tools to make it happen, what often happens is that a rational/intellectual statement of the sermon's goal becomes the preacher's attempt to accomplish the sermon's goal. The preacher tries to make the function statement happen for his listeners by speaking it passionately. So in the case of Romans 8, the preacher simply proclaims the goal in intellectual terms: "Let me reassure you, brothers and sisters: God is with you even in your greatest troubles!" What you have is a rational statement that asserts what you want to accomplish, rather than some homiletical craft that actually accomplishes the emotional/spiritual goal in the function statement. A propositional statement of our sermon's nonpropositional goals will not move us very far down the road toward writing sermons that have a full-bodied, whole-life impact.

Writers know the sort of reaction they're hoping for in their readers, whether they're trying to convince or frighten or delight. I suppose it would be of some use to fiction writers if, before they started to tell the story, they wrote down, "I want this story to frighten my readers." But will this statement of goal do much to make the story frightening? A rational statement of what your writing (or preaching) is trying to accomplish is easily produced; writing (or preaching) in such a way that a person is convinced, frightened, or delighted is the difficult part.

The Bible is a living, full-bodied book. It doesn't just speak to your head, but it also "penetrates to the point that it separates the soul from the spirit and the joints from the marrow" (Heb 4:12). The Bible cuts us to the heart. When we sit down in front of our computers on Friday, all of us who preach are trying to write full-bodied sermons that impact our congregations, and a goal or a function statement is of very preliminary use in the creation of such sermons.

Imagination: Where Change Happens

Themes and goals are essential first steps in sermon making. But the work of communicating the sermon theme and accomplishing the sermon goal means switching to a new tool, a tool that works in the place where most people are inspired and changed. That tool is the image. As we will discover, most people are changed by vision. Most people are changed by something they see.

Oprah Winfrey grew up poor in the segregated south. Born in rural Mississippi to a teenage single mom, sexually abused as a child, and shuttled between her mother and her biological father, she did not enjoy the kind of upbringing that promotes human flourishing.

But in the midst of that toxic environment, Winfrey's television became a window on a better world. As Virginia Postrel describes in her book *The Power of Glamour*,[23] every night Oprah glimpsed a distant, more perfect world on her television screen: Diana Ross singing on *The Ed Sullivan Show*, Sidney Poitier arriving at the Academy Awards ceremony. Most important of all, Oprah Winfrey saw Mary Tyler Moore.

The Mary Tyler Moore Show became Oprah's favorite. She loved the portrayal of a young, single woman working in the middle of the big city, finding her way as a professional in the male-dominated world of television. Particularly important for her was the iconic opening sequence of the show. Maybe you remember it. Mary Tyler Moore walks through the streets of Minneapolis with long, confident strides. She beams at everyone she meets while the theme song, written by Sonny Curtis, tells us that Mary can "turn the world on with a smile." There is a series of images of Mary living with effortless cheer in the midst of friends, coworkers, and children, and then the whole sequence reaches its climax with Mary standing in the middle of a busy street, spinning in a joyful circle, and throwing her hat up in the air. The song concludes by joyfully proclaiming, "You're gonna make it after all!"

Sitting in her poverty, surrounded by unreliable people, and facing an uncertain future, Oprah found this opening was more than a cheerful introduction to a sitcom; it was transformative. It was a kind of gospel message that she used to steer her life. She began to dream of working in television. She began to believe that a single girl could make it after all in the world of men, and so, by the time Oprah was nineteen she was coanchoring the news at a local Nashville television station. She was living the dream inspired by *The Mary Tyler Moore Show*. From there the success compounded so that today Oprah is one of the most powerful people in all of entertainment.

How do people change? What sort of communication cuts people to the heart and moves them into new behaviors? The story of Oprah Winfrey starts to point us in the right direction. It wasn't a theme statement or a goal statement that changed her; it was a vision. It was something that happened in her imagination. It is, of course, entirely possible that in her youth, Oprah could have stated her ambition in terms of a theme and a goal.

Theme: "Mary Tyler Moore makes me believe that the exciting life of a television newswoman is possible for me."

Goal: "I will work to become a television journalist."

But neither the theme nor the goal was the thing that caused Oprah to climb out of poverty and toward television. The vision of joyful Mary spinning in the streets of Minneapolis lived in Oprah's imagination, and that's what propelled her forward.

This goes way beyond Oprah. What Oprah's story suggests anecdotally, many modern theologians and students of human behavior suggest as theory. In his books *Desiring the Kingdom* and *Imagining the Kingdom*, James K. A. Smith has the same sense of reason's limits as I have sketched out in chapter 1 of this book. In *Desiring the Kingdom*, Smith's concern is not about preaching but rather about the related work of teaching and Christian formation. He notes that many of our attempts to form young people center around the task of passing on a worldview: "On this account the goal of a Christian education is the development of a Christian perspective, or more commonly now, a Christian *worldview*, which is taken to be a system of Christian beliefs, ideas, and doctrines." He believes that insofar as it limits itself to beliefs, ideas, and doctrines, this enterprise is basically wrongheaded:

> What if we began by appreciating how education not only gets into our head but also (and more fundamentally) grabs us by the gut—what the New Testament refers to as *kardia*, "the heart"? What if education was primarily concerned with shaping our hopes and passions—our visions of the good life—and not merely about the dissemination of data and information as inputs to our thinking? What if the primary work of education was the transforming of our imagination, rather than the saturation of our intellect?[24]

Smith is not advocating a new species of anti-intellectualism with these words. He is not saying, "Reason bad, imagination good." If he were writing to preachers, he would not say that themes and goals were useless and the imagination should get all our attention. He simply asserts that, just as the visions of Mary Tyler Moore undergirded Oprah's youthful choices and all the rational decisions that followed, so all of us build our rational choices on the foundation of our loves. In Smith's own words: "I am not advocating a new form of pious dichotomy that would force us to choose between either the heart or the mind. Rather, I will sketch an account of the priority of affectivity that makes possible and undergirds the work of the intellect."[25]

Of course, Smith isn't the first thinker to celebrate the imagination. Homileticians have long known about its centrality in human formation and its importance for the preaching craft. Thomas Troeger calls preachers to "imaginative theology," which "employs the visionary and integrative capacities of the mind to create theological understanding. It uses the powers of observation to become receptive to the Holy Spirit who works upon our consciousness through patterns of association and juxtaposition."[26] Back in the nineteenth century Henry Ward Beecher called the ability to speak to the imagination "the most important of all the elements that go to make the preacher."[27] And for the last fifty years, homiletics has been trending away from traditional homiletics, which emphasized rational dissemination of information, and toward the new homiletics, a movement that emphasizes the importance of the listener, the importance of story, and the place of the imagination.[28]

In the first book of The Artistry of Preaching series, *Preaching as Poetry*, Paul Scott Wilson explores the contours of today's postmodern mind-set, and he argues that preaching that attends to the imagination is precisely the sort of preaching needed in today's pulpits. In our context, "Reason and logic have taken a hit; they are seen as only one expression of knowledge; values and principles are favored over rules and arguments." He calls for theopoetic preaching, which he defines as preaching that speaks of God in poetic ways. "This is not preaching poems; it is poetic preaching that treasures language—with all of its frail images, symbols, and metaphors—to communicate God."[29]

Images as Agents of the Imagination

If the imagination is the place where change takes place, if it is the faculty to which preachers must appeal if they want to make their themes and goals come alive, what's the best tool for engaging the imagination and making change in that foundational place? A variety of scholars agree: stories and pictures.

In his books, James K. A. Smith marshals a wide variety of philosophers and social scientists in service of the theory that desire and imagination are what really move people, and in doing so he gives a kind of account of how the process works. He outlines three steps. First, we love. It is our desires that shape our behavior: "To be human is to love, and it is what we love that defines who we are. Our [ultimate] love is constitutive of our identity." Second, our love is aimed. Love has a *telos*. It takes the form of an intentional longing: "What we love is a specific vision of the good life, an implicit picture of what we think human flourishing looks like." Third, and most important for our purposes as we think about preaching and controlling images, these loves take the form of pictures that live in our imaginations.

> It is important to recognize that this [longed-for flourishing] is a *picture*. This is why I have emphasized that we are fundamentally non-cognitive, affective creatures . . . A vision of the good life captures our hearts and imaginations not by providing a set of rules or ideas, but by painting a picture of what it looks like for us to flourish and live well.[30]

Our deep loves steer us, and the steering happens when pictures of the good life, pictures transported by images and stories, are presented to our imagination. The French novelist Antoine de Saint-Exupéry put it more poetically. He said, "If you want to build a ship, don't drum up people together to collect wood and don't assign them tasks and work, but rather teach them to long for the endless immensity of the sea."

The church (though not all preachers) often forgets the importance of the imagination for moving and changing people. Led by moviemakers, television producers, and advertisers, the culture around us uses images and stories to move humanity, but the church lags behind. Smith quotes Michael Budde of DePaul University:

> Stories, symbols, songs, and exemplars—in our days, of course, it is not the Church that carries these to most people, even to most Christians. For people in advanced capitalist countries (and in ever-larger parts of the euphemistically labeled 'developing world'), most of their stories, narratives, images, and sounds come from centralized, for-profit transnational corporations—the so-called global culture industries.[31]

Smith then goes on to complain: "Unfortunately because the church remains fixated on content and 'messages,' it fails to see what's really at stake in these global culture industries: our imaginations. What can seem benign and safe on the Disney Channel can be a powerful co-option of imaginations for a consumerist, egocentric comportment to the world."[32] It's a fancy way of saying that we can't fight mass consumer culture and its idols with an arsenal of themes and goals; we need pictures and stories.

Images and Stories at Work

When you look around you soon realize that all kinds of images and stories are working on our imagination and shaping us in the most important areas of our lives.

Sometimes a negative image can be the source of imaginative power, as in the story of Emmett Till. In 1955, fourteen-year-old African American Emmett Till was visiting relatives in the Delta region of Mississippi. While there he was accused of flirting with a white woman, twenty-one-year-old Carolyn Bryant. Bryant's husband, Roy, and his half-brother J. W. Milam took revenge by seizing Emmett, beating him severely, gouging out one of his eyes, and then killing him. After the murder they disposed of the body by throwing it in into the Tallahatchie River bound with barbed wire and weighted down with the fan from a cotton gin.

When the crime was discovered and the body brought up from the river bottom, Emmett's mother, Mamie Till Bradley, insisted on a public funeral with an open coffin to display the brutality of the beating. At the funeral, reporters took pictures of Emmett and all the major magazines published those pictures. Images of this fourteen-year-old boy's mangled remains sparked outrage. People all over America became aware of the racism present in the country, and suddenly an issue that had flickered quietly on the periphery of the white suburban conscience became something strong and central. African Americans whose frustration had simply simmered suddenly found themselves galvanized by righteous anger and holy purpose. The civil rights movement took a big step forward, and an image of a boy's destroyed body was at the center of that movement. Before Emmett Till, many Americans had been against the abuses of racism in principle; after Emmett Till their principle burst into passionate action, and it was an image that lit the fire.

Sometimes a positive image is the driving force. Think, for example, where romance gets its power. Romantic love is driven by positive pictures dancing in the imagination. When two people are mutually besotted, they say things to each other such as, "I can't stop thinking about you." What do they mean by that? Are they talking about rational thoughts? Is the boy making logical arguments in his head where he systematically evaluates his beloved's traits, thereby forming a case for her overall excellence? Hardly. These unstoppable thoughts involve inner visions and warm daydreams. They are pictures of shared pleasures in the present and shared plans in the future. The love-struck male *imagines* the two lovers together, he imagines marrying this girl, buying a home, and raising a family. The romance is rooted in the imagination.

That doesn't mean romance is irrational. Imagination isn't opposed to reason; in fact, the two cooperate. Reason makes sure that the lover doesn't imagine logical impossibilities: he doesn't picture living with his girl in ancient Egypt or as settlers on Pluto. Reason also helps him evaluate his imaginings; after the romantic imaginings take hold, reason kicks him back a few steps to where he can evaluate his daydreams. At some point a love-struck young man must look at this relationship rationally, asking hard questions about the couple's compatibility. Imagination fuels the romance, and reason evaluates and steers. The two work together.

It's not just romantic love that works this way; imagination is a driving force in the moral life of a Christian. Agapic love depends on imagination. We will find it hard to love another person unconditionally unless we can imagine how God loves us completely even though we're a mess. Compassion also works this way. Compassion requires the ability to see what the other person is experiencing, to picture what it's like to be in his or her shoes. We overcome the fear and contempt we might feel toward a bedraggled panhandler on the streets of Chicago when we imagine what it must be like to sleep on an air duct at night and then beg for handouts all day. A failure in compassion is often a failure of the imagination.

Even the biblical description of faith shows that faith is rooted in the imagination. According to the preacher of Hebrews, those great faith champions of chapter 11—men and women like Abraham and Sarah and Moses and Rahab—were heroes of faith not because of their intellectual acumen and understanding of systematic theology but because they were "looking forward to a city that has foundations, whose architect and builder is God" (Heb 11:10). Their stories suggest that faith is more seeing than knowing. It needs knowledge, of course, but it begins in the imagination.

Again, none of this is meant to simply dismiss reason, propositional thinking, and the use of theme statements in preaching. I take imagination and reason to be partners in the gospel. They are not opponents (indeed, I'm not sure either of them ever functions without the other); they are mutually reinforcing, mutually sharpening faculties.[33] God means them to work together. Reason and imagination each approach reality from a different angle, but used together under the lordship of the Holy Spirit, they reveal to us the true meaning of things.

Preachers Reaching for the Imagination

Working preachers and homileticians have long understood that theme and goal are not enough to propel a good sermon. They understand that if they want their sermons to move people, they need more than a theme and a goal. Working preachers have always sensed that they need to find ways to touch the imagination.

Barbara Brown Taylor is eloquent about the desire to reach the imagination. In *The Preaching Life*, she writes about how it feels to write a sermon; the book is a kind of homiletical autobiography showing us her anxieties and sharing her secrets for writing a good sermon. For Taylor, speaking to the imagination is a central problem. It's so important for her that she devotes a whole chapter to it. She's convinced that a sermon starts to sing when thematic propositions blossom into something more:

> If, in the process of composing a sermon, the preacher discovers the visceral connection between the word "God" and the heart pounding experience of authentic love, the sermon will be more than correct, it will be true, not at the level of explanation, but at the level of experience, where all our deepest truths are tested.
>
> This is where a sermon becomes art. It is not enough to tell a congregation what they need to know about God, or scripture, or life.[34]

Taylor offers no technical discussion on the nature of a sermon theme, no advice about how to formulate your sermon goal; Taylor doesn't use precise homiletical terms, but her point is clear nevertheless. She says that a theme and a goal are not enough. A couple of rational statements, no matter how clear and well formulated, only get you part of the way along the path toward a good sermon.

Taylor doesn't just hold up the need for preaching art, she reflects on how that art goes for her. She talks about how she approaches her weekly text and finds the sermon's imaginative center.

> I am hoping for a moment of revelation I can share with those who will listen to me and I am jittery, because I never know what it may show me. I am not in control of the process. It is a process of discovery, in which I run the charged rod of God's word over the body of my own experience and wait to see where the sparks will fly. Sometimes live current is harder to find than others but I keep at it knowing that if there is no electricity for me, there will be none for the congregation either. . . .
>
> [Sermon preparation] is a time of patient and impatient waiting for the stirring of the Holy Spirit, that bright bird upon whose brooding the sermon depends. Over and over again I check the nest of my notes and outlines, searching through them for some sign of life. I scan the text one more time and all of a sudden there is an egg in plain view.[35]

This is a wonderful *imaginative* description of what the preaching process feels like. Most sermons that work do indeed have a moment where an egg appears in the nest of the text, something that allows the sermon to sing. But as eloquent an explanation as this is, and as nicely as it might describe the *feeling* of writing a sermon, there is something infuriatingly imprecise about Taylor's description. Waiting for an egg? Running the "charged rod of God's word" over the body of your experience? Turning the words of the Bible "loose on the events of . . . everyday life"? It all sounds great, but what does it mean? How do you do that? Is it simply a matter of waiting? This is the crucial moment, the central part of sermon preparation, and we are given no guidance about how to work this part of the sermon art, nothing beyond "wait"?

Whenever preachers talk about the imaginative portion of the sermon they seem to break into metaphor-speak. They resort to koans. They write sentences like, "We are God's impressionists."[36] They talk about "run[ning] the charged rod of God's word over the body of [their] own experience."[37] It's lovely language, but can't we be more specific? Can we offer some concrete advice on how to make the sparks fly?

It won't be easy. There's a reason why homileticians tend to wax poetic when they talk about this part of sermon preparation: because it's really hard to explain how it happens. Here's Taylor again: "All the parts of preaching can be taught: exegesis, language, metaphor, development, delivery. What is hard to teach is how to put them all together, so that what is true is also beautiful, and evocative and alive."[38]

It may be hard, but we can make progress here. Paul Scott Wilson notes that some people treat the imagination as a mysterious force that cannot be bridled or tamed; as if, when it comes to inspiration, all we can really do is sit and wait for flashing light and the angel voices. Wilson points to the work of musicians as a way to debunk this myth:

> All musicians in the symphony are artists and have imagination. And all imagination involves mystery. But the best expression of imagination, the most powerful way of disclosing its mystery, comes from learning the techniques of the instruments. Musicians have studied theory. They have learned skills. They have practiced long hours; and when it comes time to play, no matter what the innate talent of the players, the wondrous sound that is produced in that moment of time is the product of years of accomplishment.[39]

The goal of this book is to help preachers learn and practice techniques that will help them appeal to the imagination. The goal of this book is to encourage preachers to use controlling images in their sermon as a way to make their goal statements come alive and propel their sermon themes into their congregations' hearts.

Beyond Theme and Purpose: The Four Pages

So, how does a preacher speak to the imagination? How do we move beyond theme and goal statements toward practices that produce sermons that cut to the heart? Modern homiletics is increasingly concerned with this question, and homileticians have made various proposals.

One of the most imaginative contemporary homileticians is Paul Scott Wilson. Wilson's books consistently move beyond simple theme/goal language toward exploring new ways to make sermons impactful. *The Four Pages of the Sermon* is the centerpiece of these books. In it Wilson calls preachers to imagine sermons less like ideas being explained and more like movies playing in the congregation's mind. "Ever since childhood, when our family bought its first television set, I have been fascinated by movies. Movies are a symbol of our audiovisual culture, and I am finding moviemaking to be better than telling stories as an analogy for preaching."[40]

Wilson distinguishes the moviemaking task sharply from the task of essay writing, a skill most of us learned well in our academic odyssey:

As long as we prepare our sermons by conceiving of our task as equivalent to writing an essay, as typing, or perhaps even as speaking into a computer that turns our thoughts into words on a page, the essay concept will influence our preaching, often in negative ways, because we will unwittingly apply the rules of [essay] writing, which are not always effective for spoken presentations. . . . If we imagine we are directing a film we allow ourselves to think and compose sermons in a visual manner—which is how most of us think in any case . . . we will create entire worlds that address the senses, the mind, and the heart. When I speak of movie making to students in my classes and preachers around North America, I sense their own excitement at the possibilities.[41]

Clearly, Wilson is trying to write a book that helps preachers reach the imagination.

Out of this movie metaphor, Wilson proposes the four-page method of preaching. I'll explain it briefly because, when I analyze sermons, most of the language I use comes from Wilson's method. It's a language worth learning because it really does help busy preachers find their way from basic theme statements into imaginative sermons.

Each "page" of the sermon is a metaphor for one of the four sections, or four elements, that a good biblical sermon ought to have. They are as follows:

Page 1: Trouble in the Text. In this section the pastor studies the biblical text for the week in order to identify the point of trouble. What sins or miseries do God's people face in this passage? Doubt? Discouragement? Temptation? Pride? Inappropriate anger? Complacency? Fear? Scripture explores all sorts of human sin and sorrow, and every passage touches on one or more of these troubles. Section one of a sermon examines this trouble as it appears in the text and in the lives of God's people in the biblical past.

Page 2: Trouble in the World. In this section the pastor takes the trouble he or she has found in the text—let's say it's fear—and looks around his or her own world to say where that trouble manifests itself today in the lives of others, especially in the lives of God's people. What makes us afraid? When are we afraid even though we shouldn't be? When are we not afraid even though we should be? What does fear do to people, to our relationship with others, to our relationship with God?

Page 3: God's Action in the Text. In this section the pastor begins to turn to the good news of the gospel and explores how God brings salvation to the brokenness named on pages 1 and 2. How did the power of the living God address the sin and the misery of God's people all those years ago? How did God meet the fear? What divine actions or words show us how God addresses these sins and miseries and ultimately offers release from them?

Page 4: God's Action in the World. In this section the pastor talks about how the same saving action that God demonstrated back in the old days of scripture is still working today. If so far the sermon has been addressing fear, the pastor uses this page to show the congregation how God is actively casting out their fear today. God isn't someone who did a lot of cool saving stuff a long time ago; the Christian God is a living and active God who still saves and redeems and challenges our world.

This is Wilson's four-page structure; this is his moviemaking scheme; this is his language for sermon construction. It is effective in creating imaginative sermons because it forces the preacher to make comparisons and analogies. The preacher must make an analogy between the trouble in the ancient world with the trouble today, maintain the tension between sin and grace, make analogies between the work of God in the text and the work of God in contemporary lives. The imagination is engaged by comparing things usually kept apart,[42] so when Wilson calls us to pair grace and trouble, when he calls us to compare present and future, he moves us to a place where imaginative sparks can be generated.

So the four pages themselves are an excellent first step toward sermons that engage the imagination, but there's more you can do. Wilson acknowledges this. In addition to introducing the four pages, he also suggests some other preparatory disciplines that might help us write good sermons. He names six signs the preacher must heed before he or she heads onto the highway of sermon composition. Hasten onto the highway without proper attention to these signs and the preacher will lose direction. The sermon will be filled with false starts and wrong turns. The congregation traveling along will find the journey convoluted and confusing. Here are the six steps he suggests:

1. Choose one text.

2. Identify a theme.

3. Identify one doctrine associated with the text and theme.

4. Find one dominating image.

5. Recognize a congregational need.

6. Focus on one mission arising out of the text.[43]

These six steps are all important in their own way, but I would like to examine one of these steps particularly because I think it is essential to the creation of an imaginative sermon: namely step 4, the choosing of one dominant image.

The Importance of a Controlling Image

While he thinks they're important, Wilson does not think a controlling image is central to the creation of an imaginative sermon. Here's how he describes its use: "A dominant image in a sermon is a repeated image, and when listeners see it over and over, it begins to stand out in their minds. . . .

Listeners should see the same image in a sermon introduction, on one or two other pages, and in the conclusion."[44]

So far, so good. I like this description very much. But Wilson goes on to minimize the significance of the unifying image: "Such an image is not essential for each sermon; a sermon can function quite well without one even as any sermon might be enhanced by having one."[45] He also suggests that you needn't choose such an image early on in your sermon preparation. In many cases this one image doesn't become clear until you're working on the end of your sermon; an image hits you and so you go back and work it through the whole thing.

I agree that an image does sometimes come late in the writing process, so late that you have to retrofit the rest of the manuscript, but this is certainly not ideal. In the interest of creating imaginative sermons, I would like to hold out for selecting an image up front. If a sermon is going to engage the imagination, it will need a guiding image to keep the listener's imagination focused. Just as a theme is crucial for keeping the sermon rationally on track in the mind of the listener (making sure the sermon doesn't stray in the rational realm), so a central sermon image is crucial for keeping the sermon on one imaginative track so that it is clear to the heart of the listener (making sure it is clear in the realm of the imagination). Or to borrow the hard-chair/soft-chair language of Fred Craddock: if the sermon theme is the one-sentence statement that comes out of your hard-chair study, the unifying image is the one picture that centers your soft-chair work.

Everyone agrees that you need a sermon theme to make a sermon work; I think a unifying image may be as important as a clear theme. Have your image clearly identified at the beginning of the sermonic process and the writing will be more sharply focused right from the beginning, your listener will be able to track with you in heart as well as mind, and you will be ready to make a vibrant sermon out of the beautiful mess.

A Tool for Imaginative Preaching: The Controlling Image Statement

So rather than settling for a theme and a goal, I would like to suggest that preachers add a third statement to their list: a controlling image statement. As I said earlier, a controlling image is an evocative picture or scene that shows up repeatedly in a sermon. It communicates either the trouble or the grace of sermon theme and therefore helps to accomplish the sermon's goal. This statement should be one sentence long, it should fit with the sermon's theme and goal, and it should provide the congregation with a phrase or a picture that captures either the sin or the grace of the Bible passage.

Here's how that might look for a sermon on Romans 8:18-27, that rich passage that refers to creation's groaning and the Spirit's interceding for us as we ourselves groan like women in labor. A fair theme passage would be: "The Holy Spirit helps us in times of trouble." It's a nice sentence, if not all that inspiring. But what if we added an image to that theme? If our groans are the groans of labor, maybe we can think of the Holy Spirit as our midwife, helping us toward new birth. Now we have something that will stick to the imagination. If that's our chosen path, our three statements would look something like this:

Theme: The Holy Spirit helps us in our times of weakness and trouble.

Goal: To help God's people push through their times of weakness and trouble.

Controlling Image: The Holy Spirit is like a midwife who groans beside us as we live through the birth pains of the new creation.

If they want to write sermons that linger in the minds of their hearers, preachers will find that adding this statement of controlling image will help them immensely.

Good preachers, experienced preachers, probably do this already. They may not write down an image statement, but in their sermon preparation they search for an image to spark and center their work, and the moment that the image emerges out of the beautiful mess is the moment that they finally feel ready and even eager to write.

Last year around Easter time, I was in conversation with my friend John Rottman, who teaches homiletics at Calvin Theological Seminary. He was preparing to preach on Luke 24:13-35, the story of the Emmaus road appearance, in a church on a Sunday just after Easter. John had preached on the passage before but he wanted to write a brand-new sermon for the occasion. His exegesis was done and he was brooding over the beautiful mess of accumulated insights and observations. I asked him how the process was going and he, with some degree of enthusiasm, said, "It's going well. I think I know where I'm going. In verse 21 the two men say about Jesus 'We had hoped he was the one who was going to redeem Israel.' I like that phrase, 'we had hoped.' It makes you think of all the lost hopes of people everywhere. I think I'm going to focus on that."

After John had pored through his exegetical treasures, this was the image that stood out to him: this picture of two men trudging down the road, referring to their hopes in the past tense: "We had hoped." He felt as though this was an image he could build a sermon around. "We had hoped" is a universal cry; all people have been in that place where hopes suddenly feel past tense. And the gospel hope of Jesus's resurrection is an exhilarating answer to this universal sadness. That moment when John identified this image was absolutely central to his sermon-writing process. It was the moment when he knew he didn't just have a text but a sermon.

If you talk informally with good preachers about how a sermon comes together, they will describe a similar moment when some particular insight or angle that sums up the whole text gels in their hearts and minds and suddenly they are ready to write. Whether or not they realize it, most of the time that catalytic insight, that energizing angle, comes in the form of a controlling image or a centering phrase. Without that imaginative spark, it's hard to start writing.

Controlling Images:
A Field Study

All this talk about images sounds great in theory, but what does it look like in practice? We have defined a controlling image as *an evocative picture or scene that shows up repeatedly in a sermon, that communicates either the trouble or the grace of the sermon theme and thereby helps to accomplish the sermon's goal.* Does such a tool actually work? Over the arc of our lifetimes, we've heard and read a lot of great sermons; did they use controlling images? If all our sermons anchor themselves in a controlling image or phrase, will all our sermons start to look and sound the same? Are we locking ourselves into a single form?

In this chapter we will answer these questions by looking at how images function in real, published sermons. We will see how controlling images allow the preacher to turn a propositional theme statement into a vibrant sermon that speaks to the imagination as well as the rational mind. We will see that controlling images are powerful tools because they transform sermons that simply teach and inform into sermons that move. I hope we will also see that images are flexible tools. When a preacher decides to look for a controlling image or phrase for the sermon, he or she is not locked into one form. It's my contention that a sermon of just about any form is improved when it engages the listener's imagination with a controlling image.

Much of this chapter will use other people's sermons to make this point. I don't know how each of these preachers arrived at their controlling images; they probably didn't write them down as statements before they began. But because I am interested in finding disciplined ways to touch the imagination, because I think that writing down a controlling image statement might be a practical way to make any sermon more imaginative,

I will conclude each sermon example with a speculative guess at what the three statements of the sermon might be. I will conclude each example with a theme statement that briefly states in active language the central theme of the sermon, a goal statement that states what the sermon intends to accomplish, and the controlling image statement, which will propel the theme sentence by evoking either the trouble addressed by the text or communicating the grace it brings. Perhaps that will help you to imagine how your own controlling image statements might be formulated.

An Example of a Controlling Image

Let's make sure we're clear about what we mean when we talk about controlling images. Most sermons use metaphors and analogies, and all beginning preachers are encouraged to use concrete visual language in their sermons. So, for example, a three-point sermon on God's love may compare God's love to a flowing river to illustrate its healing qualities, to a mountain to emphasize its enduring qualities, and to a "dying" seed sown in the ground to emphasize its sacrificial qualities. These are fine examples of imagery used in a sermon, and they may well be effective in illustrating each individual point, but they are not controlling images.

A controlling image is something more substantial. A controlling image doesn't just illustrate a single point or a single section of a sermon; it anchors all the points, it grounds the narrative flow, it appears on all four of the sermon's "pages." Wilson's definition is a good one: "A dominant image in a sermon is a repeated image, and when listeners see it over and over, it begins to stand out in their minds. . . . Listeners should see the same image in a sermon introduction, on one or two other pages, and in the conclusion."[1]

It's not just the frequency of a controlling image that distinguishes it; it's also the depth. A good controlling image doesn't just illustrate an idea but also represents a bigger reality. It points beyond itself. A good controlling image or phrase aims for the resonant power of myth rather than the didactic power of illustration. While an illustration helps a listener understand a concept (an indispensable tool), a good controlling image propels a sermon; it causes the pathos of the human condition or the joy of God's grace to resound in a listener's heart.

So a preacher might use the image of a rabbit ears aerial on a television to illustrate faith: through faith we receive God's constantly transmitting grace just as the rabbit ears on a TV set receive a station's constantly transmitted signal. That's a fine illustration. It helps makes one aspect of faith clearer. But it doesn't have the deep resonance of a controlling image.

A controlling image for a sermon on faith might be the words of the man who wanted Jesus to cast a demon out of his son: "I have faith; help my lack of faith" (Mark 9:24). Or it might be the picture of the woman with the flow of blood, an untouchable desperate for healing, reaching out in the middle of a crowd to touch the hem of Jesus's robe. These are more than illustrations, they are pictures of what faith looks and feels like. They are images of the reality of faith. They don't just explain; they have resonance. So a good controlling image will have both frequency and depth.

Barbara Brown Taylor's sermon "None of Us Is Home Yet"[2] is a good example of a preacher using a controlling image that has both frequency and depth, resulting in a sermon with resonance and power. The sermon is based on Matthew 6:25-26, the section of the Sermon on the Mount where Jesus tells his followers not to worry about the things of this life: "Look at the birds in the sky. They don't sow seed or harvest grain or gather crops into barns. Yet your heavenly Father feeds them. Aren't you worth much more than they?" Taylor uses the image of home to anchor this sermon. We are driven by a desire for home. It's because we desire a secure home that we are tempted to spend all our time gathering and reaping and storing up in barns, that we are so restless in this life, and that we hunger for God who is our true home, our true rest. The image pervades the sermon and shows up in all of its main sections.

It starts in the introduction where Taylor tells the story of going to a house blessing at which Matthew 6 was read. Jesus's words end up upsetting our notions of what makes a home:

> "Therefore I tell you, do not worry about your life, what you will eat or what you will drink, or about your body, what you will wear. Is not life more than food, or the body more than clothing?" The words fell like stones in deep water. No one coughed or cleared a throat as Jesus preached to us, assuming that we believed him, assuming that we took God's providence for granted. He was telling our friend that she was safe, but not because she had a roof over her head and a key to the front door. "You are safe," Jesus told her, "because God who made you will not abandon you. That is your home, which nothing and no one can take away from you."[3]

With this story, and particularly with this paragraph, Taylor takes a familiar image, the image of our home, and makes it stand for a larger world.

She uses it to raise questions about where our security lies; she uses it to suggest a different kind of home from the one we're used to worrying about.

Later in this sermon Taylor uses home as an image that represents our search for security and peace:

> Home. What a compelling, elusive word that is. What a strong hunger the human heart has for home, and what a hard thing it is for the human heart to find and keep a home—not just a building, but a place to belong.[4]

In the middle of the sermon she shows how biblical characters were people on a pilgrimage looking for home:

> For as long as God's people can remember, they have been seeking the way home. "A wandering Aramean was my father . . ." That is how the story of Israel begins in the book of Deuteronomy, and that is the story every Hebrew learned to repeat when presenting first fruits to the Lord. However settled God's people became, however prosperous they became, in their promised land, they were not to forget the long roundabout journey by which they had been delivered there. Wanderers once, they would be wanderers again, but wherever they went they were to remember: their destination was never Egypt or Jerusalem or Babylon, but God.[5]

Toward the end of the sermon the image appears again, this time as an illustration of how our deep longings for fulfillment and security are never quite realized in this world:

> On any given night, however comfortable we may be and however secure our futures may seem, we remain vulnerable to a certain heaviness of heart that can come upon us for no apparent reason at all. It may begin as a flutter in the chest or as a full-blown ache—a sudden hollowness inside, a peculiar melancholy, an inexplicable homesickness. Have you felt it? The sense that there is a place you belong that you have somehow gotten separated from, a place that misses you as much as you miss it and that is calling you to return, only you do not know where or how to get there.[6]

After some reflection on the places we wander in search of home and the ways we go wrong looking for false security, the image of home comes back as grace at the sermon's end. Here is the very last sentence:

We can serve the God who feeds and clothes and shelters us by doing some of that ourselves, but always with the knowledge that it is God who provides—no—who is our true and only home, in whose household there is plenty—for the birds of the air, for the lilies of the field, and for every one of us.[7]

I don't know if Barbara Brown Taylor wrote down a theme, a goal, and a controlling image statement before she started writing. She probably didn't. But if she had they would have looked something like this:

Theme: God provides for all his wandering people.

Goal: To move restless Christians to find their rest in God.

Controlling Image: Home. All the restlessness of God's people is really a yearning for the one who is our true home.

You'll notice I couldn't help stating the theme and the goal in terms of the controlling image. I used the word "wandering" in the theme and "restlessness" in the goal. Both of these metaphors orbit around the central image of home. To get a sense of how the image is crucial to the process, imagine the theme and goal stripped of their connection to the central image:

Theme: God provides for his people.

Goal: To have people trust God's provision.

The poverty of these two sentences is obvious. They are true, but they are also terribly bland. Compare them to the relative piquancy of the theme and goal informed by a controlling image and you begin to see how important the controlling image is.

"None of Us Is Home Yet" is a textbook example of how an image can center and propel a sermon. It not only connects this sermon to Taylor's theme but also provides a tool for her to speak not only to the people's rational minds but also to their imaginations. The image doesn't just illustrate some abstract point Taylor is trying to make; it is a resonant image: home has all sorts of deep associations and feelings attached to it; it has mythic weight. Used in the hands of a brilliant preacher like Taylor, this image makes for a full-bodied, effective, affective sermon.

Controlling Images:
Both Static and Kinetic

So far we've talked about sermons centered on images, that is, sermons centered on a picture or occasion that is primarily visual in nature. In the example just cited, *home* is a visual image, a physical place, a place we can all picture in the mind's eye. Other physical, visual objects that might give a sermon an imaginative center include the cross or the open grave. These images are static.

Sometimes, however, the centering image can be kinetic. The preacher can center the whole sermon on a particular event rather than a particular object. Just as a gripping scene from a movie might jolt your imagination, the preacher might choose a whole scene as a centering device. So, for example, Paul and Silas singing hymns in the darkness of the Philippian jail might be the center of a sermon on Acts 16, the whole scene and not just one object from it (the dark, the song, the shackles). Moses's going against God's orders, striking the rock in a moment of frustration and pride, is a scene you could use as a controlling image to center a sermon on Numbers 20. Whether moving or static, some sort of physical picture presented to the mind's eye is one way, perhaps the primary way, to center your sermon.

Here's a good example of a controlling image that is really a centering scene. A pastor named James Rose preaches a sermon on David and Goliath. Rose uses the scene of Goliath striding up and down the valley of Elah, taunting the Israelites, as the visual center of his sermon. At a literal level, the taunting giant is obviously the physical embodiment of the trouble that faces David at that moment in his life. But Rose broadens the scene into a controlling image. It's not only David who faces taunting giants; it's Israel; it's us.

> Giants are overwhelming for those who look at life from that level. Giants are terribly hard to handle on your own. Israel ought to know: they've had troubles before. The report of Goliath's imposing ancestors stopped a whole generation of Israel at the door to the Promised Land . . .

Rose goes on to talk about how, viewed from ground level, the giants faced by Israel seemed menacing and invincible, how Caleb and Joshua were the only ones brave enough to take them on. Then, having established the image of Goliath looming over Israel, and having shown how the giant was an archetype of Israelite fears, he broadens the image even further by moving it into the present day.

> [Giants] roam in every generation—theirs at 1000 B.C. in Elah Valley and ours at A.D. 2000 in our valleys. I'll bet you've got one in your valley, a valley you must cross, if you're going on with God. I do, too. My giant has been waving at me lately.[8]

This engaging image opens up all sorts of homiletical possibilities. You can use the image of facing giants at the ground level to describe the trouble side of the text (Wilson's pages 1 and 2). That's what we have in Rose's paragraph. The taunting giant is used as an image to describe all the "giants" that have faced God's people throughout our generations. The taunting giant becomes an effective metaphor for the power of evil in general.

You can even see how the giant image could become a reference point for the grace portion of the sermon (Wilson's pages 3 and 4). When you talk about people who feel overwhelmed by their giants, the good news could be articulated using the controlling image. There are all sorts of ways you could do that. For example, instead of facing the giant from ground level (from a human point of view) as Israel did, you could explore what it would be like facing the giants from God's perspective, as David did. As a person of the resurrection, you could remind the listeners about how God defeated the giant of death also by moving a stone.

If James Rose had simply written down a theme for his sermon on 1 Samuel 17, it would probably be something like this: "God overcomes big enemies using small people with ordinary means." That's a fine theme, and it communicates an important biblical truth. Heaven knows, hundreds of sermons have been written on the foundation of this theme. Preacher after preacher has told us about God's sovereign power and how God is able to work that power through the Davids of this world. Those sermons are solid, they are true, they are gospel, but they are not particularly memorable. It's the physical imagery of the taunting giant that propels this rational truth with sufficient velocity to hit us right between the eyes, to cut us to the heart.

If James Rose had written down all three of our proposed centering statements at the beginning of his sermon process, it might have looked something like this.

Theme: God overcomes big enemies using small people with ordinary means.

Goal: To encourage people to see their giants from God's perspective.

Controlling Image (in this case a controlling scene): A taunting giant. We all deal with giant problems that seem way beyond our size and strength. These giants taunt us as we try to live our lives.

Again, I think you can see that it's the image that takes the thematic idea and makes it into a vibrant sermon.

Sermons Propelled by
Controlling Phrases[9]

So a visual image—moving or static—is one tool the preacher can use to imaginatively center a sermon, but it's not the only tool. Sometimes a sermon can center itself around a compelling phrase. A pithy line from the text, or a memorable phrase composed by the sermon author can be repeated throughout the sermon. This repetition not only helps center the mind; like a repeated chant it also penetrates the heart, the imagination.

In one of my classes a student preached on Romans 8:18-25, the part where Paul talks about all creation groaning, waiting for its redemption. At the beginning of her sermon she gave examples of the groaning of creation drawn from the Bible and everyday life. She finished every example with the phrase, "Can you hear the groaning?" At the end of the sermon she brought the gospel to bear on creation's groaning. She spoke of how the groaning was expectant, not hopeless; she spoke of the Spirit's work in bringing forth the new creation; she laid out some real-life examples of hope still singing out in the midst of groaning. She finished every one of these gospel words with the phrase "Can you feel the hope?" It wasn't a visual picture; it was a phrase; nevertheless, it had both frequency and depth, and it still centered the listener's imagination.

My colleague's sermon on Luke 24:21 centered on the disappointed words of Cleopas and his companion as they walked the Emmaus road: "We had hoped." There, too, the sermon is using a phrase as its imaginative center.

A more extensive example of this technique is found in Martin Copenhaver's published sermon "Forsaken with Jesus."[10] Copenhaver's sermon text is Mark 15:29-34, the story of Jesus's crucifixion, and he centers the sermon particularly on the phrase, "My God, my God, why have you left me?" the words Jesus quoted from Psalm 22 when he was in his deepest agony.

Copenhaver begins the sermon by wondering what Jesus could have meant by these words, and he reviews some suggestions made by various interpreters. Some people say Jesus didn't seriously doubt God's presence; when he cited Psalm 22:1 he meant to refer to the whole psalm and all the listeners who heard him speak those words would have known that Psalm 22 ends in triumph for the psalmist, so clearly, they say, this is not a cry of abandonment; it is a cry of victory.

Copenhaver also mentions others who focus on the "my" of "My God, my God." Jesus was still a believer even when in pain because "the God who is absent is still '*My* God, *My* God.'"[11] Jesus was still expressing deep faith.

While he expresses sympathy with these interpretations, Copenhaver finally goes beyond them. He believes that Jesus felt abandoned, and he uses the phrase to explore not only how suffering felt to Jesus but also how it feels to you and me. These words become more than words on Jesus's lips: they become the cry of all humankind.

> "My God, My God, why hast thou forsaken me?" It is the cry of those who wonder how it is that circumstances seem to conspire against them. . . . It is the cry of the patient clutching the sheets of the hospital bed, the cry of the prisoner in Auschwitz."[12]

Copenhaver finishes the sermon by saying that this cry of Jesus shows suffering humans that Jesus shares the most desperate times of our lives. The good news of this sermon is that Jesus crouches with us in the darkness.

> "My God, My God, why hast thou forsaken me?" It is difficult to let those words stand, raw and not explained away, yet there are gracious benefits in doing just that. . . . He came to live among us, not as God in a human costume . . . in Jesus God came as human to the bone.[13]

It's a phrase that controls this sermon and carries the imaginative impact. The phrase has both frequency and depth. It's the first word of Copenhaver's sermon and it appears at the head of every major section. It focuses the listener's mind, to be sure, but ultimately, as we see the sense of the phrase expanded, it cuts the listener to his or her troubled heart.

If I were to attempt a summary of Copenhaver's three statements, it would look something like this:

Theme: Jesus is with us in our deepest troubles.

Goal: To comfort hurting and frightened people.

Controlling Phrase: "My God! My God! Why have you forsaken me?" A genuinely frightened and hurting Jesus groans this universal cry as he crouches in the darkness with us.

While both controlling images and controlling phrases are useful tools for appealing to the imagination, there are certainly differences between them. Generally speaking, an image is a better tool than a repeated phrase. Imagery is the imagination's natural language, so when a preacher speaks in pictures he or she has the most direct access to the listener's imagination. Nevertheless, a controlling phrase is sometimes the best choice.[14] Certain texts don't lend themselves very well to imagery—many Pauline passages, for instance. Paul was not afraid to use imagery, and when he used it, he used it memorably: "We have this treasure in clay pots" (2 Cor 4:7), "Run in such a way as to get the prize" (1 Cor 9:24 NIV), "Now you are the body of Christ, and each one of you is a part of it" (1 Cor 12:27 NIV), "Present your bodies as a living sacrifice" (Rom 12:1). Some of the best and most enduring biblical images come from Paul's pen. Nevertheless, most of Paul's writing is neither narrative nor poetry—genres that are more visual and image-saturated; most of Paul's writing is in the mode of rational persuasion, and sometimes the most effective way to center a sermon based on Paul is through a phrase rather than an image.

It should also be said that the best controlling phrases have a cache of strong images attached to them. Copenhaver's "My God, my God, why" evokes Christ's suffering on the cross. Martin Luther King Jr.'s repeated phrase "I have a dream" evokes specific pictures that King painted in his speech, pictures of what his dream looked like: slaves and slave owners sitting down together in brotherhood and little black children and little white children joining hands. So even when a sermon is anchored on a controlling phrase, concrete images are not far off.

Sermons Propelled by Controlling Images from Outside the Biblical Text

Another nuance in the way controlling images and phrases are used involves the sources of these images. Where do preachers find their centering images? If you read good sermons you notice that preachers dig them up from different places—they are not restricted to biblical texts.

Sometimes they get their phrase or their image from outside the biblical text. Frederick Buechner's sermon "Message in the Stars"[15] is a wonderful example of how a controlling image allows a sermon to speak to the imagination as well as to the head. In this case the source of the image is Buechner's own fertile imagination. His sermon theme could be summed up rather easily, maybe something like: "God speaks to us in our daily lives through our small choices, in our crises, and even in our longings." It's a popular theme for Buechner. He often calls people to listen to their lives so that they can hear God speak. Good advice, and much needed for today's people.

Yet this theme, as good as it may be, does not anchor this sermon, and if we were to ask Buechner to name the point at which this sermon found its center, he might not point to the identification of his theme. This sermon is built around a controlling image, the image of a message written in the stars.

As a counterpoint to the ordinary, daily speech of God that fills our lives, Buechner imagines what it would be like if God spoke in a different way. What if God laid aside all subtlety and signed his name in the heavens?

> Suppose, for instance, that God were to take the great, dim river of the Milky Way as we see it from down here flowing across the night sky and were to brighten it up a little and then rearrange it so that all of a sudden one night the world would step outside and look up at the heavens and see not the usual haphazard scattering of stars but, written out in letters light years tall, the sentence, I REALLY EXIST.[16]

Buechner goes on to play with this imaginary occurrence. Initially people would fall to their knees and be terribly impressed, he says, and the churches and synagogues would overflow. But eventually, after a couple of years, the novelty would wear off and people would go back to their regular business: "And in the twinkling of an eye the message would fade away for good and the celestial music would be heard no more, or maybe they would continue for centuries to come, but it would no longer make any difference."[17] Grandiose displays of presence are not what we need, says Buechner, and neither are we much helped by cosmic propositions, however glittering their presentation may be. What our hearts crave is something very different:

> For what we need to know, of course, is not just that God exists, not just that beyond the steely brightness of the stars there is a cosmic intelligence of some kind that keeps the whole show going, but that there is a God right here in the thick of our day-by-day lives . . . It is not objective proof of God's existence that we want but, whether we use religious language for it or not, the experience of God's presence. That is the miracle we are really after. And that is also, I think, the miracle that we really get.[18]

From there Buechner goes on to describe some of the ways we experience God "here in the thick of our day-by-day lives."

You can imagine a sermon based on the same theme as "Message in the Stars" constructed in a completely different way. The preacher could start out with a general story of how much we need God's presence in our lives and then move on to three places where God does speak to us.[19] That would be a fine sermon, but not a memorable one. Because Buechner uses the message in the stars as a controlling image, he creates a memorable sermon.

Here is my attempt to summarize the three statements associated with "Message in the Stars":

Theme: God speaks to us in our daily lives through our small choices, in our crises, and even in our longings.

Goal: To help people see a living God beside them in their lives.

Controlling Image: A message in the stars. People's indifference to the stars looks like modern people's indifference to distant propositions about God and old miracles.

You can clearly see how Buechner's controlling image comes from outside the realm of biblical text. Is this OK? Both in terms of word count and in terms of the impression it leaves on the imagination, the controlling image in this sermon takes up a good deal of sermonic space. Can Buechner's sermon be biblical when he centers so much of the sermon on material from beyond the text?

I think it can. Even though Frederick Buechner uses an outside image, he is using it in a way that captures one of the main concerns of his text, Philippians 3:12–4:7. To use the four-pages sermon language, he uses this image to summarize the trouble in the text and in the world. The trouble in the text for Philippians 3:17ff is Paul's imprisonment in Rome. Paul is under house arrest, he's been in custody for a long time, and he's not sure whether he will live or die. Under such circumstances a normal person would be asking himself, *Is God really near, or has God abandoned me?* The parallel trouble in the world would then be something like the following: *Life is hard. Is God there? I'm slogging through a lot of crud; is God present in any of this?* That's certainly the question Buechner tries to address in this sermon. He might have tied his imagery more explicitly to the text, but still, it seems to me that the image of the message in the stars is an effective way to capture the text's central trouble.

Buechner's sermon shows us that controlling images from outside the text can effectively propel a gospel sermon. Imaginative preachers soon learn that the wide world provides an endless supply of images that could propel a sermon. Movie scenes, local events, congregational stories, national news stories, world events, sporting contests—compelling, resonant images regularly appear in all these places.

Sermons Propelled by Controlling Phrases from Outside the Biblical Text

In her sermon "The Bottomless Glass,"[20] a sermon based on the wedding feast at Cana in John 2:1-11, Fleming Rutledge also looks outside the text for a controlling device, but she chooses a phrase paired with a controlling image.

Again, the theme of the sermon is fairly easily stated: "Jesus fills the deep needs of his people when nothing and no one else can." This is a solid theme, and I think it's pretty clearly derived from the text. Actually, as themes go, it's on the imaginative end of the spectrum. You could imagine a preacher choosing a theme like "Jesus shows the disciples his glory by changing water into wine," a theme that would be true but not very interesting. At least Rutledge's theme comes from an engaging angle.

Nevertheless, by itself, even this angular theme is not what makes this sermon work. Rutledge propels this theme into the imagination of the listener with a centering image. Out of all the images and concerns of the text, she directs us to one moment in particular: the moment when the party runs out of wine. She captures that moment with a phrase that she imagines on the lips of the party's host when he realizes the wine is gone: "Is that all there is?" That disappointed phrase ends up representing not only the problem of this first-century wedding reception; it also becomes the cry of late twentieth-century emptiness: the wine has run out; is that all there is? Rutledge uses this phrase (she uses "Is that all there is?" and "There should have been more to it all" seven times in this sermon) to tie the trouble in this text to the trouble of our modern western world.[21] Once the trouble is established she presents the grace in the text—the miraculous provision of new wine—in terms of this phrase. The theme is an important exegetical summary of the text, but the controlling phrase makes the sermon work.

Notice that this phrase comes from outside the text. It is the title of a popular 1969 song by Peggy Lee. Nowhere in the Bible story does the host of the party stand over his empty wine bottles, asking, "Is that all there is?" Rutledge takes the textual fact of a wedding that's run out of wine, and then she imagines what that might have looked like: "In today's reading from John's gospel, we discover Jesus at a wedding where the wine has run out. We *can imagine* the dismayed host saying, 'Is that all there is?'"[22] Even though this phrase is from outside the text, it still leads to what I would call a biblical sermon. That's because it clearly and explicitly summarizes the trouble in John 2 and so paves the way for the grace that this passage proclaims. The controlling phrase is from outside the text, but it is rooted in the text and so the overall effect is an augmentation of the Bible's message rather than a distraction from that message.

Here is my rendering of the three statements for "The Bottomless Glass":

Theme: Jesus fills the deep needs of his people when nothing and no one else can.

Goal: To have people turn to Jesus to have their thirst quenched.

Controlling Image (in this case anchored by a phrase): "Is that all there is?" Our relentless human thirst leads all of us at different points in our lives to ask, "Is that all there is?" Only Jesus's fabulously abundant wine is sufficient to meet those thirsts.

Sermons Propelled by Controlling Images from Within the Biblical Text

Walter Brueggemann shows us a different way of using controlling images in his sermon on Exodus 11:4-8, 12:29-32 entitled "The Midnight of Power and Weakness."[23] Instead of coming up with a phrase or an image from his own imagination, Brueggemann takes an image from the Bible itself.

Exodus 11–12 describe the story of the tenth plague, that terrible night when every firstborn in Egypt was killed by the destroyer and Israel was finally released from her slavery. Brueggemann distills this complex story down to this fairly simple theme: "God's gracious and uncontrollable power defeats the exploitative, imperial power of Pharaoh through the weakness of Israel." I think that's a pretty good exegetical summary of what this text is about. That's a good hard-chair statement of the text's message.

But once again this theme is not the center of the sermon. The sermon is propelled by a vivid image. Brueggemann starts with this rich, expansive biblical story with all sorts of events and details, and he settles on one small detail as his homiletical center. The sermon revolves around that remarkable moment in the middle of the night when Pharaoh, the most powerful man in the world, comes to poor Moses, the former Midianite shepherd, and begs Moses to bless him. Here's how Brueggemann describes that moment:

At midnight Pharaoh is able to see the surge of life to which he has no access. In this awesome reversal of imperial policy, there is Pharaoh's series of imperatives that concedes everything. The Pharaoh issues one more stunning imperative, one of the most astonishing utterances in all of human history. After Moses had for so long addressed truth to power, now finally, pitifully, power speaks to truth. Pharaoh feebly says to departing Moses, "Bless me, be a blessing to me, bless me as well!"[24]

This really is a remarkable moment,[25] and Brueggemann frames it brilliantly. He not only uses it as a way to sum up this particular story but also holds it up as an archetype: This is how the Lord God of Israel does things in this world! This is the shape of Christian experience through history!

Brueggemann brings other great moments in redemptive history into orbit around this central picture of Pharaoh pleading for a blessing from Moses: "David before Nathan, Zedekiah before Jeremiah, Pilate before Jesus, Agrippa before Paul, Charles V before Luther, Hitler before Niemoeller, Wallace before King, Husack before Havel."[26] He culminates the sermon with the picture of the power of the cross conquering the world through weakness and the affirmation, "The more blatant forms of power must come finally, just after midnight, and say 'Bless me.' The story of Pharaoh is the story of failed power; the story of Moses is about unnoticed but irresistible possibility. The story is played out just after midnight."[27] Here then is a summary of theme, goal, and image in this wonderful sermon:

Theme: God's gracious and uncontrollable power defeats the exploitative, imperial power of Pharaoh through the weakness of Israel.

Goal: To help God's people to persevere in the "weak" power of Christ rather than give in to (or adopt) the imperial power of Pharaoh.

Controlling Image (in this case a scene): Pharaoh kneeling before Moses at midnight, asking for a blessing. The ultimate triumph of God's grace is all captured here.

The theme of this sermon is critical to keeping the text biblical and theologically on track, but it is not enough to create a vibrant sermon. The controlling image propels the sermon and makes it sing.

Unlike Buechner and Rutledge, Brueggemann gets his image right out of the text. Pharaoh asking Moses for a blessing at midnight is not something he has to import; it's right there.

Comparing Inside and Outside Images

Controlling images and phrases taken straight from the text have some advantages over those brought in from the outside. First, and most important, they rigorously ground the sermon in scripture. There can be no doubt that the exegetical and the creative portions of a sermon are working together with the creative part flowing out of the exegetical part. Second, when the controlling image of the sermon comes from the text, the listener is given the ability to hear scripture in a whole new way. After reading Brueggemann's sermon, I can't imagine reading through Exodus 11–12 without noticing the power of Pharaoh's midnight plea, and when I see Pharaoh before Moses my mind will be transported to the midnight glory of the cross. A passage of scripture has come alive for me.

In the case of Buechner's sermon, where the controlling image is completely manufactured, and even in the case of Rutledge's sermon where the controlling image is a moment imagined by the preacher within the narrative of the biblical story, I'm not at all certain I will think of their words when I read the Bible passages again. Next time I read the miracle of the wedding feast at Cana, will I imagine the host saying, "Is that all there is?" Maybe, but probably not. And when I read Philippians 3:12–4:7, will I remember that this is the text upon which Buechner based his famous sermon, "Message in the Stars"? Almost certainly not.

I once heard a sermon on envy in which the preacher used the image of a bowl full of ice cream to evoke the sin of envy. He recalled the way he and his siblings would invidiously compare the size of their ice-cream portions as soon as their mom put their dessert on the table. Instead of finding pleasure in the yummy ice cream in front of them, they found misery in the extra tablespoon of ice cream in a sibling's bowl. It was a great evocative image. I still remember the message of the sermon vividly, but I can't for the life of me remember what text the preacher was using.

None of this means images from outside the text are bad. It's simply a recognition of the sorts of factors involved when you choose your controlling image. While it may not help listeners to remember the preaching text because it comes from the contemporary world, an image from outside the text might be more immediate to the listener and carry stronger emotional associations. An image from within the text might help listeners remember the Bible passage that grounds the sermon, but it may not have the resonance of a gripping story from the news or a poignant moment from a well-known film.

In October 2014, Paul Scott Wilson preached a sermon just a week after Canada was shaken by a shooting in Ottawa, the nation's capitol. Corporal Nathan Cirillo, a soldier keeping watch at the National War Monument, was gunned down by a self-styled jihadist. The whole country was shaken and sobered by the incident. Canada thinks of itself as a peaceful nation, and the incident led to national soul searching. In the wake of this tragedy, Wilson used a news story that emerged after the shootings to express the theme of his sermon on Matthew 22:34-46: "God's consistent message to us in all the seasons of our lives is a message of love."

> Barbara Winters, a lawyer and former medical assistant in the Canadian Armed Forces naval reserve, was one of five people who rushed to the side of Corporal Nathan Cirillo and tried to keep him alive after he was shot at the National War Monument this week. She gave CPR while another corporal who had been on guard gave mouth to mouth resuscitation, and then they switched positions. "'There was no panic, there was no screaming—everybody was just focused on the soldier and trying to help him,' said Winters . . . [who] moved to Cirillo's head while the other man took over chest compressions. She watched as the colour went back into his face, but he soon began to grow pale. She began telling him how loved he is and how proud everyone is of him. 'I kept telling him repeatedly that he was loved, that he was a brave man,' said Winters through tears. 'I said look at what you were doing—you were guarding the dead. You were standing at the cenotaph. I said we're all so proud of you, your parents are so proud of you, I said your family loves you, everybody here that's working on you loves you.'"
>
> Those may have been the last words he heard. I believe that Barbara and the others would not have been able to do their good deeds if God had not empowered them to do so. Barbara's words to Cirillo are God's words to us in each moment, I love you, you are so loved.[28]

Even far removed from the event, the image of this woman speaking words of love to a frightened young man has power, but delivered to a Canadian congregation a week after the event, it would have had enormous imaginative force. Such are the advantages of controlling images from outside the text: they have great propulsive power and they bring the sermon into the world of the listeners. A careful preacher can effectively use them as long as he or she makes sure the biblical text is not eclipsed by their power.

There are advantages and disadvantages to both kinds of controlling images. Part of the craft (and the joy!) of preaching is learning to balance these considerations as one puts together the sermon.

Controlling Images Should Center on Either Trouble or Grace

As I mentioned in chapter 1, because I am associated with a seminary where Paul Scott Wilson's *The Four Pages of the Sermon* is the central text, I am used to talking about sermons using the terms *trouble* and *grace*. To review quickly, Wilson divides a sermon into four "pages," page 1: trouble in the text; page 2: trouble in the world; page 3: God's action in the text; and page 4: God's action in the world. So pages 1 and 2 of this method are concerned with life's trouble, and pages 3 and 4 are concerned with God's grace (God's action). Whether or not you know Wilson's book, whether or not you're comfortable with the four-page terminology, I think it's fair to say that every sermon that empowers through the good news—in one way or another—uses these two categories. In every sermon there is some tension, some imperfection, some problem that needs to be addressed (trouble), and in every sermon the preacher must offer some movement of God that addresses the problem with saving action (grace). Good preachers propel their sermons forward through the interplay of trouble and grace.

This distinction between trouble and grace gives us another lens with which to examine the use of controlling images in sermons. When we read good sermons that employ controlling images, we find that they work best when the preacher chooses an image to represent either the trouble in the sermon or the grace of a sermon. If the image used only captures some small subpoint, if the image is used to illustrate one part of the sermon's application, it will not be, it cannot be, a *controlling* image. When an image is used repeatedly to sum up the trouble of the people in the biblical text and the trouble facing God's people today, or if the image is used to illustrate the amazing action of God revealed in the text and still present in our lives today, it can propel the sermon.

Furthermore, even though a controlling image will be either an image of trouble or an image of grace, the image should show up in both the announcement of trouble and the proclamation of grace. If the controlling image is a picture of human misery, the gospel must show us God overcoming that misery using terms from the metaphorical world of the trouble image. So, for example, if your controlling image is darkness, announce your gospel as light. Conversely, if the controlling image proclaims grace, the trouble in that sermon should be described with metaphors that anticipate the coming grace and complement it: if your controlling image is the shining of the light, describe the trouble as darkness.

To illustrate the truth of this, let's return briefly to the sermons already cited in this chapter, sermons where controlling images are used effectively, and we will see how each preacher uses a controlling image to represent either trouble or grace, and sometimes both.

In the sermon we just examined we noted how Walter Brueggemann used the moment when Pharaoh begs departing Moses for a blessing as the centering image of the story. This scene clearly captures the grace of the sermon. It is the moment when power bows to truth; it is the moment where the world is stood on its head and the last are first and the first are last; it's a moment that anticipates the resurrection of Jesus Christ; it's a moment when God's action is clear and attractive. And a brief review of the end of his sermon reminds us that Brueggemann means to stir our hopes by this image: "The more blatant forms of power must come finally, just after midnight, and say 'Bless me.' The story of Pharaoh is the story of failed power; the story of Moses is about unnoticed but irresistible possibility. The story is played out just after midnight."[29] In Brueggemann's sermon, the controlling image stands for God's action, God's grace.

Frederick Buechner's "Message in the Stars" uses the controlling image to summarize the trouble. Buechner tells the story of God writing a message in the heavens in which he proclaims, "I REALLY EXIST," only to have his message ignored and dismissed by a busy, skeptical world.[30] He uses this story to illustrate a fundamental problem in our lives, our inability to know God's presence and our particular inability to read the more grandiose signs of his presence. The story of the message in the stars acknowledges the trouble of our separation from God and our general inattention to him.

Later in the sermon Buechner responds to this trouble with the good news, and he does it in the terms of the trouble image. He suggests that God's grace is best seen in small, intimate places where quiet acts of love and kindness continue to speak God's name, rather than in distant proclamations of existence. Again the image anchors the sermon, but this time it does it by capturing the trouble.

The first sermon we looked at in this chapter was Barbara Brown Taylor's "None of Us Is Home Yet." Taylor does something a little different again. The image of *home* clearly governs that sermon and *home* is clearly an image of grace. It's an image that sums up the peace and safety of being brought finally into God's household after a lifetime of searching and wandering. As Taylor finishes the sermon she uses this image as a way to summarize God's saving action: "We can serve the God who feeds and clothes and shelters us by doing some of that ourselves, but always with the knowledge that it is God who provides—no—who is our true and only home, in whose household there is plenty—for the birds of the air, for the lilies of the field, and for every one of us."[31] This is the good news. God is our true home.

But Taylor also uses this image to capture the trouble of her sermon. At the sermon's beginning, instead of accenting the grace of our future homecoming with God, she accents our lack of a home, our homesickness. So the image centers the trouble, too:

> On any given night, however comfortable we may be and however secure our futures may seem, we remain vulnerable to a certain heaviness of heart that can come upon us for no apparent reason at all. It may begin as a flutter in the chest or as a full-blown ache—a sudden hollowness inside, a peculiar melancholy, an inexplicable homesickness. Have you felt it? The sense that there is a place you belong that you have somehow gotten separated from, a place that misses you as much as you miss it and that is calling you to return, only you do not know where or how to get there.[32]

Home is an image of grace, but Taylor manages, to good effect, to use the image in both the trouble and grace portions of her sermon.

We also sampled the sermon by James Rose on David and Goliath. The controlling image there was *taunting giants*; Goliath the giant was made to stand for all the giant troubles that face us in our lives. Here the application is very clear. *Giant* is a symbol of trouble in the text and in the world. Rose invites the listeners to think of their problems as giants so that at the end of the sermon they can imagine how God helps them to defeat the giants coming down into the valley to meet them. It's a very clear, very effective example of an image used to summarize the text's trouble.

Fleming Rutledge's "The Bottomless Glass" centers the listener on an imagined moment when the host of John 2 finds out the wine is gone and asks himself, "Is that all there is?" That phrase becomes the center of her sermon and stands not only for the consternation of the wedding host but also for the consternation of all those modern folk who find out that their lives are empty and the party's over. Clearly it's another image for trouble. We are invited to see all our disappointments and regrets in the words of the disappointed host.

Finally, as an example of a controlling phrase as opposed to a controlling image, we also looked at Martin Copenhaver's sermon on Mark 15. He centered his sermon on the phrase, "My God, my God! Why have you left me?" Again, the preacher takes this expression of abandonment spoken by Jesus on the cross and makes it stand for the anguished cries of all the abandoned; in other words the controlling phrase stands for the trouble of the sermon: "'My God, My God, why hast thou forsaken me?' It is the cry of those who wonder how it is that circumstances seem to conspire against them, and who begin to believe that God is in on the conspiracy."[33] At the end of the sermon Copenhaver announces the good news of the gospel in terms of the trouble summed up in the controlling phrase: "'My God, my God, why hast thou forsaken me?' It is difficult to let those words stand, raw and not explained away; yet there are gracious benefits in doing just that. A Jesus who would experience the full range of human circumstances and human emotions must surely experience the sense of being forsaken."[34]

Again the image works because it captures one of the two major components of the sermon, in this case the trouble.

Based on these examples, controlling images are only really effective when they summarize the sermon's trouble or grace. That shouldn't surprise us. The trouble and the grace are the two moments in the sermon when the preacher has the opportunity to cut the listener to the heart. If you find a sermon grabbing you, chances are you are either moved by the depth of your broken condition, or you are moved by the amazing grace of God shown in the Holy Spirit through Jesus Christ our Lord, or better still, you are moved by both. So, naturally, it is precisely at this point, when heart and mind need to be engaged, that the application of a good image is the most needed and the most effective.

Controlling Images and Sermon Tone

I have been arguing that you can use a controlling image to represent either the trouble or the grace of a sermon. Is one to be preferred over the other? Is it better to let your image stand for God's gracious action rather than let it represent the broken human condition?

Paul Scott Wilson thinks so. He tentatively suggests that preachers should choose controlling images for God's grace and should avoid images that represent sin.[35] He suggests that if you use a strong image for sin, it will weaken the good news of God's grace. The sin will stick in the imagination, the grace will be forgettable.

I think Wilson is right to be concerned about sin's overwhelming grace. It's a danger in any sermon. After all, don't people prefer Dante's *Inferno* to the *Purgatorio* and the *Paridisio*? Don't people always say that the devil is the most interesting character in Milton's *Paradise Lost*? Doesn't the prevalence of bad news on our evening newscasts testify that bad news gets higher ratings than good? We must always be on our guard against sermons that lay out the tragedy of human sin with dramatic verve and then make the good news of the gospel seem predictable and dull.

Nevertheless I think Wilson is wrong to suggest that controlling images that center on grace need to be preferred. Images can summarize trouble without eclipsing grace. As long as the saving action of God on pages 3 and 4 is announced in terms of the controlling image on pages 1 and 2, the grace will still shine.

James Rose's sermon on David and Goliath, the one studied earlier, is a good example of what I mean. The controlling image in this sermon is the taunting giant Goliath. Rose makes the mocking Philistine a symbol for all our fears and troubles that slouch out of the valley to taunt us as we try to live our lives. It's clearly a controlling image centered on human sin and misery. However, this tragic image doesn't need to eclipse the grace. If the preacher concludes the sermon by announcing how on the cross Jesus defeated the giant of death by moving a stone, he does not diminish the grace with the image; he uses the image to actually allow grace to shine more brightly. When he announces the grace in terms of the trouble image, it's as though the darkness of the trouble sets the grace in relief. It's like a Rembrandt painting where most of the painting is dark, but a shaft of light illuminates one central object.

Here's Rembrandt's painting of an old man. The painting is dark except for the old man's hands and his face.

Rembrandt, *Portrait of an Old Man in Red*, Hermitage Museum, Saint Petersburg, Russia.

The beauty of the man's hands and face are not diminished by the painting's relative gloom; in fact their beauty is enhanced.

While controlling images for grace and for trouble are both permissible, it does make a difference which one you choose. It's a decision about the tone of your sermon. In music a composition has a different feel depending on what key it's written in. Songs and symphonies in a major key are brighter, more positive, more upbeat works; those written in a minor key have a sadder, more restless tone. A preacher has some of the same tonal control when choosing where to apply the controlling image. If the preacher chooses to use an image that represents trouble, the sermon will be slightly darker, more Lenten. If he or she chooses an image that summarizes the gracious action of God, the sermon will have a brighter feel, maybe something more appropriate for Easter. In that respect a controlling image can become one of the exciting tools a preacher can use to fine-tune his or her messages.

Conclusion

We've reviewed many sermons in this chapter and covered quite a lot of material. All of it strongly suggests that controlling images work. All of it strongly suggests that when a preacher stands over the beautiful mess of exegesis, after centering the ideas with the theme statement and identifying what he or she wants the message to do by writing the sermon goal, he or she will take a large step toward a vibrant and impactful sermon by adding a controlling image statement that evokes the sermon theme with a compelling picture of the sermon's trouble or the sermon's grace.

What Preachers Can Learn from Poets

We've seen how great preachers use controlling images across a whole range of sermon forms, and we've seen how those images can propel a good sermon. In this chapter we will shift gears. If, as we have been saying, imagery is so important for sermons, if a good image helps make a sermon impactful and memorable, where can we preachers go to learn more about how images work? Are there other masters who use images, who study how they work, and who know the value of controlling images in particular? Who might help us hone our craft?

The poets might help us. Preachers have used images over the years, but when it comes to choosing and molding a metaphor, we are rank amateurs compared to poets. Poets have been working with images from the beginning. As long as poetry has existed, men and women have been trying to find good metaphors for their compositions. As long as poetry has existed, men and women have been trying to understand how images work and where their power comes from. If we preachers want to write sermons that use controlling images effectively, we could learn a thing or two from the poets.

In this chapter we will step out of the realm of homiletics and into the world of poetics. We will explore how images work in poems. We will listen to poets reflecting on why images are important and what makes them powerful. We will see how poets use controlling images in their writing. Then after spending time in the poetical realm and learning from these experts, in chapter 4 we will step back into the homiletical realm and try to apply what we've seen to our sermon writing.

Luminous Detail: Poets Using Images

Maybe you're not convinced that writing poetry is analogous to sermon writing. Maybe you think sermons and poems are completely different things. Let me try to convince you otherwise. Poetry and preaching do have differences—we'll deal with some of those differences later—but in some basic and important ways there are real similarities.

Poets and preachers face similar challenges. Like preachers, poets start with a beautiful mess, all of it collected from their textual observations. Of course their messes come from a different text. While preachers compile their messes from reading and studying a Bible passage, poets make their messes by examining the world around them. A poet's text is life and all its stuff: relationship dynamics, natural phenomena, personal feelings—the poet is constantly looking at all of these for inspiration. Every day as the poet reads the paper and mows the lawn and talks to colleagues and buys the groceries and takes children to piano lessons, the poet will observe a thousand remarkable things happening in the world. All of them may be interesting to the poet, but to make a poem he or she must somehow choose one bit of experience, one image, one incident from the beautiful mess and make it sing. Somehow one small portion of life, one small observation of the world is made to stand for more than itself. Or to put it in the words of poet Mary Oliver: "What is poetry but, through whatever particular instance seems to be occurring, a meditation on something more general and more profound."[1] So just like preachers, poets find one image in the beautiful mess and they use it to propel their work.

That's what happens in Robert Frost's famous poem "Stopping by Woods on a Snowy Evening." I urge you to find a copy of it so that you can clearly see how Frost takes an image, a moment, a small observation of the world, and turns it into a meditation on something more profound. As the title suggests, the moment around which the poem centers is a man pausing in a New England wood on a snowy night. He's sitting on a horse-drawn cart, and he's obviously in the middle of some sort of pressing errand, but in the midst of that errand, the loveliness of the wood and the quiet beauty of the snow overwhelm him, and he stops, transfixed. Frost's use of language in describing the moment is so masterful that the reader feels the same expansive sense of awe that the rider has as he watches the woods fill up with snow.

The poet takes that well-drawn image and turns it toward the profound with the poem's famous ending. Just as both reader and rider are feeling the deep peace of the woods, the duties of life come crashing in. Frost ends the poem with the words "But I have promises to keep, / And miles to go before I sleep."[2] "And miles to go before I sleep" is repeated at the poem's conclusion, like a wistful refrain.

Through Frost's craft this ordinary moment becomes something that stands for more than itself. The quietness and beauty of the moment, the serenity of the snow-filled woods is contrasted with the relentless pull of the man's duties and all of a sudden this simple moment stands for something bigger; it becomes representative of life's nagging incompleteness. There is joy in the world, but it is fleeting. Beauty soon gives way to duty and demand. We are not home yet; we are not at rest.

This very concrete image taps into the depth of human existence. Frost's controlling image so effectively captures how life feels for people that almost a hundred years later Frost's poem is still recited, taught, and beloved. People still read it and say, "Yes, that's what life is like. Life is like stopping in the woods on a snowy evening."

The image propels the poem. If Frost had tried to elicit a sense of the unfinished nature of life by talking about it directly, the poem probably wouldn't have worked. If he'd said, "My oh my, life is hard and our work is never done. We have no time for beauty and joy," the words would have been true, but forgettable. It's hard to get at these deep feelings directly. But when a poetic image is used, the mind expands, the heart springs open, and the image sticks.

The dynamic is at work in another one of Frost's poems, "Nothing Gold Can Stay." This poem takes a different image at its center. This time Frost turns his poetic eye toward a simple, straightforward item, a sprouting plant, and he makes it stand for something more.

We've all seen how a plant's early spring growth has a sort of golden color. If we've grown up in the northeastern United States, we all know that in the spring the trees flower before the leaves come out green, and many of these trees have a kind of golden flower. The flowering doesn't last long. After a week, the delicate buds give way to the sturdy leaves. Most of us see this happen every year and we think nothing of it; or if we do think of it, we think of it in botanical terms.

But Frost sees that brief golden moment, that momentary flowering, as an image for the fleeting beauty of youth and innocence. The poem's title is a kind of theme statement. Just like the golden flowers, all beautiful beginnings are doomed to decay. Youth will give way to old age. The hopeful dawn will become the mundane day. Frost even widens the focus of the poem to include the fall of humankind as "leaf subsides to leaf, / So Eden sank to grief."[3] "Nothing Gold Can Stay" is eight lines long. It has only forty words, and no word is more than two syllables. And yet with amazing efficiency, propelling the poem with a single image, Frost has managed to evoke a deep sense of creation's travail. And please notice, he hasn't just said it; he's *evoked* it. I challenge anyone to use basic prose to accomplish the same thing in forty words. It can't be done. Poets know the power of images.

A Poem's Trajectory: From Delight to Wisdom

How do poets harness the image's power? They start with a blank sheet of paper and the sprawl of personal experience; out of this beautiful mess, how do they manage to pluck one perfect image around which to build a poem?

It's not easy. Poets are hunters, looking for a phrase, a picture, a newspaper headline, an evocative moment that will sprout into a poem. They prod the beautiful mess of their experiences, turning over rocks, combing the dark corners of their attics looking for something that will take hold of their imaginations.

Sometimes the search can be long. Just as preachers will tell you that the hardest part of preaching is moving from the beautiful mess of exegesis to the specificity and structure of a good sermon, so poets will tell you that plucking a meaningful image out of the mess of their experiences is really difficult. Both poets and preachers find a blank sheet of paper intimidating.

Poet David Citino admits to being intimidated. He thinks that grabbing something out of the beautiful mess of your experience is definitely the hardest part of writing a poem, much harder than all the other technical aspects.

> Line breaks, rhythms, exigencies of form. A sonnet? That's easy. Fourteen lines of iambic pentameter. It's when we try to talk about the creation, the willing into existence of something palpable and living where before we could detect only blank space, the white page or the blank screen, that we find ourselves with a severe case of aphasia, or at least a prolonged spell of hemming and hawing.[4]

Prolonged spells of hemming and hawing. What preacher can't identify with that? We may have lots of information in front of us, we may start with a pile of good exegesis but that doesn't make it easy. Just ask poets Ted Kooser and Steve Cox:

You are bombarded every moment with sensations—the sight of a cereus blossom on your morning walk, the sound of a curve-billed thrasher's call nearby, the taste lingering from breakfast, the smell of a creosote brush, the touch of a warm sweater on your arms—so many sensations that you may feel overwhelmed. Again, were do you begin?[5]

Fortunately, poets do more than hem and haw in answer to this question. As they describe the process, finding and using that one perfect image seems to involve three steps: seeing, specifying, and going deep. Together these three steps describe a trajectory, a path; the poem and its imagery propel first the poet, then the reader, on a kind of journey. We can map that journey: a good image takes the reader on a journey that begins in delight and ends in wisdom.

The language of "delight to wisdom" comes from Robert Frost. He said that this was "the figure a poem makes," which was his attempt to describe the way a poem propels the reader.

> It begins in delight and ends in wisdom. It begins in delight, it inclines to the impulse, it assumes direction with a first line laid down, it runs a course of lucky events, and ends in a clarification of life—not necessarily a great clarification such as the sects and cults are founded on, but in a momentary stay against confusion.[6]

Preachers would benefit from following a little behind the poets and watching to see how they make this journey from delight to wisdom, because this isn't so different from the figure a sermon makes. We, too, want to communicate wisdom. We want to offer our listeners a (hopefully more than momentary) stay against confusion. Our attempts to communicate a sermon theme are pretty close to Frost's desire to bring a "clarification of life," and we also want to do it in a way that delights.

Let's follow the poets down the path and see what we can learn.

Step One: Delighted Sight

The journey begins with sight. Read poets on poetry and you are forever hearing about how the poet sees. This isn't seeing in the ocular sense—the poet isn't calling on aspiring poets to visit the optometrist—this is poetic seeing, imaginative seeing. Here are Cox and Kooser again:

> You are always drinking in the world. All writing begins with that—with your five senses. You write about what you see, hear, taste, smell and

touch. And effective writing begins with seeing the world clearly—so said the English poet John Ruskin. "Hundreds of people can talk for one who can think," Ruskin said, "and thousands can think for one who can see."[7]

Because they are so concerned about seeing, poets become people who literally walk around looking for images. They are collectors of moments and impressions that seem to have depth and meaning. In her poem "Elegy," poet Natasha Trethewey describes going trout fishing with her father, who was also a poet. It's meant to be a social trip; their relationship is a little tense and the time spent fly-fishing in the river is supposed to ease the tension. But on the trip Natasha finds that her poetic habits of seeing are so deeply engrained that the scenery of the river and the distraction of the fishing are nowhere near enough to turn off her poetic sight. Her relationship with her father is tense and awkward, and as he casts, the slice of his fishing line cutting the air between them suddenly becomes a poetic image. It symbolizes what divides them. When the image strikes her, she takes out a notebook and records it, planning to use it in a poem someday, an elegy she would write after her father's death. This seeing is a habit for her, just as it was for her dad, and the poem that finally emerges from the experience acknowledges how this habitual seeing has become almost an obsession. "I tried to take it all in" she writes, because "I was that ruthless."[8]

Any preacher who has been through the weekly grind of sermon production can identify with this ruthless obsession. The discipline of delivering a message every week changes the way we look at the world. We don't see the way everyone else does. The things we read in books, the conversations we have with friends, the stories we read in the newspaper, the events we see on our television screens: it's all potential sermon fodder. We see the world through sermon eyes. We are always on the lookout for material. We walk around searching for moments where either the desperation of the human condition or the transcendent power of God is revealed, and when we see these moments, most of us have developed ways to record them for future use. We are that ruthless.

Poet David Citino gives a good summary statement of why he is always on the lookout for images. When you find just the right image it is luminous. Luminous detail is

> that image that suggests so many others because it is connected some-
> how to the world, the universe, the collective experience of any number
> of people. We can make a list of all the images we remember in eighth
> grade, and try to fit as many as possible into a poem (the multitudinous
> method), or we can try for those few that glow with connections, that

suggest others (the luminous method). So many lasting poems are made of recollected, luminous detail.[9]

How do you know when you've seen a detail that is "luminous"? How do you know when you've seen a detail in the world or in a Bible text that has the power to become a strong sermon image? One way is to make the distinction between *denotative* and *connotative imagery.* This is an important distinction for poets, preachers, visual artists, and anyone else who wants to work with images.

Images function at two different levels. The first level is the denotative. Every image has denotative power: it stands for something specific. The red octagon denotes stopping. A flag with stars and stripes denotes the United States of America. The cross stands for the sacrifice of Jesus. When we speak of denotative meaning we are talking about an image's straightforward meaning.

But most images do more than communicate a straightforward meaning; most images also bring up feelings and associations. They have a kind of emotional punch. That's the connotative side of an image. As poets John Ciardi and Miller Williams put it, "Images denote certain sensory (usually visual) identifications *and* they connote an emotional aura."[10] The stars and stripes evoke feelings of patriotism. The cross of Christ evokes a mixture of gratitude for what Christ did and sorrow for my sins. Connotative meaning is more difficult to pin down than denotative meaning. Everyone agrees that the flag of the United States denotes the country, but we can be less sure about what it connotes in people. For a decorated veteran it may bring a mixture of pride and patriotism intermingled with sadness as he or she thinks of friends lost in combat. For the privileged teen it may only bring a low-grade patriotism tied to the material privileges he or she enjoys. For a person from another country who, for whatever reason, doesn't like what America stands for, the flag could connote imperialism.[11]

Preachers must become sensitive to the connotative part of an image if they want to use controlling images effectively. Recall that we defined a controlling image as an *evocative* picture or scene that shows up repeatedly in a sermon. It's the connotative meaning that makes an image evocative, that gives an image its power and depth. Connotative meaning is what propels an image and makes it interesting. If an image has weak connotative associations, it won't be very propulsive. A stop sign is an image with a weak emotional aura. We all know what it means, but it doesn't connote very much. It would be a mediocre image for a poem or a sermon. The kind of details that poets and preachers see are rich in connotative meaning.

So the journey of an image in a poem begins with a moment of delighted[12] seeing, a moment where the poet is struck by a luminous detail, full of connotative meaning.

Step Two: Luminous Specificity

Once the image is seen, the poet begins to work the image. This is the second step of the journey, and specificity is critically important here: the poet sees something angular and interesting and then describes it in specific detail.

Ezra Pound famously offered this advice to aspiring poets: "Go in fear of abstractions."[13] Preachers should be afraid of the same thing. Pound was trying to tell writers that broad, conceptual verbiage is the enemy of good writing. Writing that sticks is specific. Writing that sticks paints a picture. When a poet sees something luminous, he or she can't just describe it generally but must learn to describe what he or she sees in its concrete particularity.

Why must a poem begin in careful observation of something specific? Because it's specifics that engage our imaginations. In his book *The Poetry Home Repair Manual*, Ted Kooser shows how an image opens up an idea, how it touches the imagination.

> You're talking to someone who says, "Those were the good old days," and you ask, "What was so good about them?" and they say, "Well, I don't know, I guess we had a lot of fun" and you say, "What kind of fun?" and they say, "Oh, you know, family picnics and holidays." And you say, "Give me an example of something that happened at a family picnic," and they say, "Well OK . . . I remember when one time Aunt May used termite powder in a layer cake, thinking it was sugar." At that point the conversation begins to get interesting.[14]

You can't begin to write a poem if all you have is an abstract point you want to make. Sentences like "Life is short and we ought to enjoy it" or "Love is made up of actions, not lots of words," say something good and true about life, they are clear and easy to understand, but they don't cut to the heart. Ted Kooser puts it this way:

> I can't speak for all the poets writing today, but I suspect that the freshest, most engaging poems most often don't come from ideas at all. Ideas are orderly, rational and to some degree, logical. They come clothed in complete sentences, like "Overpopulation is the source of all the problems of

the world." Instead poems are triggered by catchy twists of language or little glimpses of life.[15]

Poems start with little glimpses of life and the delight that accompanies those glimpses. They develop when we explore those glimpses and describe them in thoughtful specificity. Kooser says, "Let yourself play with whatever you observe. Describe a boiling pot on the stove, the flash of bicycle spokes. What you think and feel about the world can be trusted to surface."[16] In other words, once the image strikes you, let it play in your imagination, and then build your poem around the specifics of that detail. Go in fear of abstractions.

Even though it's not a poem, the power of specificity is illustrated by this poetic obituary that was written in 2013 and then widely distributed on the web.

> If you're about to throw away an old pair of pantyhose, stop. Consider: Mary Agnes [Pink] Mullaney. . . . We were blessed to learn many valuable lessons . . . during her 85 years, among them: Never throw away old pantyhose. Use the old ones to tie gutters, child-proof cabinets, tie toilet flappers, or hang Christmas ornaments.
>
> Also: If a possum takes up residence in your shed, grab a barbecue brush to coax him out. If he doesn't leave, brush him for twenty minutes and let him stay. . . .
>
> Go to church with a chicken sandwich in your purse. Cry at the consecration, every time. Give the chicken sandwich to your homeless friend after mass.[17]

This delightful obituary goes on to tell readers about cold drinks left for the mailman, pictures of children and grandchildren shared with complete strangers in checkout lines, strangers invited to thanksgiving dinner. We hear how Pink used to put food-resistant children in laundry baskets, tell them they were lions in a cage, and then feed them through the slats. We hear how Pink never said a mean word about anybody and how even difficult people were just "poor folk to pray for."

It's the specificity that makes this obituary so wonderful. The author could have said that Mary loved animals, but how much better to tell us that she once stroked an invading possum for twenty minutes with a barbecue brush? The author could have said that Mary was thrifty, but how much better to tell us that she used old panty hose to childproof cabinets and tie up toilet flappers? The author could have said that Mary was generous, but how much better to tell us that she carried a chicken sandwich in her purse when she went to church so she could give it to her homeless friend? These aren't just details, they are luminous details. They evoke. They connote. Their specificity begins to suggest things beyond themselves.

Step Three: Speak Wisdom

We've already begun to touch on the third stage of the journey. First, the poet is delighted by something he or she sees, then specifically describes it in luminous detail, and now the image opens up and points beyond itself to some deeper truth or some deeper feeling. So, for example, in the obituary just cited, the description of Mary Mullaney's life is evocative. The details of her generosity, her kindness, her thrift are first delightful, and they engage us with their specificity, but ultimately they point beyond themselves and begin to suggest something deeper about what a good life might look like. The images are propulsive. They look deeper beneath the surface of things and begin to make us think deeper thoughts about the shape of the world and our lives in it.

As I said earlier, Robert Frost sums up these three stages (and emphasizes the final stage) when he talks about "the figure a poem makes," which is his language for the journey on which a poem propels the reader. He said that a poem "begins in delight and ends in wisdom."[18]

You can see that journey from delight to wisdom taking place when you look at the poem cited at the beginning of this chapter, Frost's "Nothing Gold Can Stay." The poem begins in delighted seeing; in this case Frost is delighted by the fact that the first color that shows on the branches of the trees around his home in the New England spring is not green but gold. Frost describes that first gold in its specificity (its brevity, its floral character), and then finally at the poem's conclusion, the poem broadens out into wisdom: Frost offers us a reflection on youth's brevity and the fallenness of creation.

This ability to propel a reader on a journey from delight to wisdom is part of the unique power of images. Ezra Pound has a slightly more technical description of the journey. He doesn't talk about the journey from delight to wisdom; instead he describes how a single image can blow open the doors of both the intellect and the emotions:

> An image is that which presents an intellectual and emotional "complex" in an instant of time . . . It is the presentation of such a "complex" instantaneously which gives that sense of sudden liberation; that freedom from time limits and space limits; that sense of sudden growth which we experience in the presence of great works of art.[19]

Poet Robert Lowell offers a more colloquial description of the journey in an interview he gave with *The Paris Review*. Again, he says that it is an image that propels the poem. At the very end of his interview, Lowell is asked, "Don't you think a large part of [writing a poem] is getting the right details, symbolic or not, around which to wind the poem tighter and tighter?" Lowell replies,

> Some bit of scenery or something you've felt. Almost the whole problem of writing poetry is to bring it back to what you really feel. . . . You may feel the doorknob more strongly than some big personal event, and the doorknob will open into something you can use as your own. . . . Some little image, some detail you've noticed—you're writing about a little country shop, just describing it, and your poem ends up with an existentialist account of your experience. But it's the shop that started it off.[20]

The same trajectory is there. You start with the doorknob or the country shop and you end up in a broader place, namely with "an existentialist account of your experience." Under the curation of the poet, the image takes you on a journey from delight to wisdom.

Please notice: the wisdom that comes at the end of the journey starts to sound like a theme. Poets don't want to start with the abstraction of a theme, but both Frost and Lowell want to move toward it. They will resist stating the theme plainly, but they do want to say something about life that could be expressed thematically. In fact, when Frost concludes his poem on the transient beauty of youth with the line "Nothing gold can stay," he's coming pretty close to offering us a theme sentence, but the theme is so much more memorable and impactful because we came to it through the doorway of delight and along the trail of specificity.

Poets and Preachers: Parallels and Differences

I hope the analogy with preaching is clear here. In most of our best sermons our listeners have been on that same journey. The sermon writing process began with some bit of the biblical text that, in Lowell's words, we feel strongly; something that delights us. We sit down at our computer and, with the Spirit's help and with lots of prayer, we work hard to share that delight with our congregation by describing what we've seen in its concrete specificity, and if things go the way we hope, by the end of the sermon, the sermon will take them on a journey toward wisdom, toward the sermon theme.

We, too, search for an image "around which to wind" the sermon "tighter and tighter." We, too, take an individual image like a doorknob or a little country shop or Jacob limping against the sunrise or dying Moses staring westward from Mount Nebo toward the promised land, and from that single image, we move toward something larger: not the "existentialist account of your own experience" that Lowell aimed for but rather a larger account of God working his purposes out in this world. A sermon moves from the delight in something specific in the text to the universal wisdom of the gospel.

Of course, preaching is not *exactly* like writing poetry as Lowell describes it. We don't simply start with an image and see where it leads. Poets tend to begin without any notion of theme whatsoever; all they have is a single vivid image. They take this image and they just start writing and see where the muse leads them. The image primes the pump of the imagination and, once the pump starts cranking, who knows what might flow? The poet could start with the memory of trying to eat melting ice cream on a hot day and end up with a poem that reflects on the transience of life, or the poet could find himself or herself with a poem that celebrates the joy of childhood summer afternoons. The theme comes at the end—ultimately the poet does want to tell you something that could be stated in a single sentence[21]—but this theme is derived from the image by way of the free imagination.

Preachers don't work quite this way. Preachers start with a text and a theme and bring the image in afterward. You can't just grab any old biblical image that captures your attention and start writing. A sermon that begins with the fatted calf of Luke 15, and, steered by the preacher's imagination, ends up in a broad reflection on the place of food in the life of God's people is not a biblical sermon. The scripture text, and our grammatical, historical exegesis of it, disciplines our imagination. Our sermonic playground is wide, there's lots of room for us to experiment, but our playground does have a fence, defined boundaries that limit the imagination's play.

In spite of these differences, the similarities are striking. When it comes to putting pen to paper (or fingers to keyboard), when it comes to actually constructing the sermon, we preachers, just like Robert Lowell, are looking for an image or a phrase to capture our theme. Once we've found it, we wind our sermon tightly around this vivid image, so that our sermon won't simply convey solid information about God; it will take us on that journey from delight to wisdom.

And that's the most important parallel between poetry and preaching. The journey from delight to wisdom is a good description of the bridge we try to build from a sermon theme—a bit of wisdom that summarizes the action of God in the text—to a sermon that makes something happen in our listeners' hearts. In every sermon we are trying to bring the gospel both as delight that touches listeners' emotions and wisdom that feeds their minds. The poets show us that there is a way to connect delight and wisdom, and the connection is made through luminous, connotative images. By showing us this connection the poets have shown us a way in which we can make our sermons more impactful.

Chapter Four
Learning from Marketers and Visual Artists

Poets aren't the only ones who know how to use an image. There are others who understand how an image can get hold of ordinary people. Ordinary people like Mabinty Bangura.

When she was only four years old, Mabinty Bangura saw an image that changed her whole life. At the time she was living in an orphanage in Sierra Leone. The civil war there had decimated her family and left her locked in poverty and hopelessness. Her father had been murdered, her mother had starved to death, and, up to that point, the only images that filled her life were images of violence and want. Even compared to other orphans' situations, Mabinty's life seemed unpromising. Her skin was covered with the white patches caused by vitiligo, and the other orphans called her a devil child.

But one day the wind blew a western magazine against the fence of her orphanage. In that magazine's glossy pages, Mabinty found an image that pierced her imagination: "There was a lady on it, she was on her tippy-toes, in this pink, beautiful tutu . . . I had never seen anything like this—a costume that stuck out with glitter on it. . . . I could just see the beauty in that person and the hope and the love and just everything that I didn't have."[1]

This poverty-stricken child was so smitten, she ripped the photo out of the magazine and hid it in her underwear. Every night, in an exercise that was almost devotional, she would take the image out of its hiding place and gaze at it. *This is what I want to be,* she thought. The image of the glittering ballerina with all her grace became an inspiration to her that "represented freedom, it represented hope, it represented trying to live a little longer."[2]

An American couple adopted her and changed her name to Michaela DePrince. Michaela settled in New Jersey where she showed not only passion for being a ballerina but also talent. And in 2012, when she was only seventeen years of age, Michaela signed a contract with the Dance Theatre of Harlem as a professional ballerina. It was a twelve-year journey, all propelled by an image.

Poets aren't the only ones who know how to work an image. Today some of the great image masters work in the world of advertising, fashion, and moviemaking. Images are the *lingua franca* of all these ubiquitous forms of communication. The people who make movies, design fashion, and devise marketing campaigns spend their days thinking about how to make visual presentations that move others, that inspire, that arrest our attention and cut us to the heart. Can these people teach us something about how to use a controlling image? Can we sit at the feet of these artists and learn from them?

It's unusual company for preachers. Especially when it comes to advertisers, we pastors spend more time fulminating against their work than learning from it. That's understandable. Consumerism might be the greatest idol of our time and these men and women are like the high priests of the idol's false promises.

Nevertheless, these people know their craft and watching them work can help us in two ways. It can help us understand how we are being manipulated by the images they present, and it helps us learn how we can counter their images of consumerism with winsome images of the gospel.

When Jamie Smith discusses the power of imagination and desire in his books *Imagining the Kingdom* and *Desiring the Kingdom*, he doesn't just talk about how the gospel works on our imaginations; he spends a good deal of time examining the work of advertisers and moviemakers, showing how they aim at the imagination too. In fact, a big part of his argument is that while we in the church have been busy trying to form the next generation through teaching them a worldview communicated through doctrinal truths (aiming at their heads), the rest of the persuaders in this world have been using images to win our children's hearts.

For example, when Victoria's Secret tries to sell its lingerie to women (and, unfortunately, also to twelve-year-old girls), it doesn't offer a set of well-reasoned arguments about why every woman needs lacy things in her underwear drawer; instead it appeals to female desires. This marketing "is communicated by very affective, visual means: tiny narratives packed into images that appeal to our faculties of desire and inscribe themselves into our imagination. The secret here is an industry that thrives on desire and knows how to get it."[3]

64

Here is Smith's extended critique of the church's approach to forming the next generation as opposed to Victoria's Secret's approach:

> A common "churchy" response to this cultural situation runs along basically Platonic lines: to quell the raging passion of sexuality that courses its way through culture, our bodies and passions need to be disciplined by our "higher" parts—we need to get the brain to trump other organs and thus bring the passions into submission to the intellect. And the way to do this is to get *ideas* to trump *passions*. In other words, the church responds to the overwhelming cultural activation and formation of desire by trying fill our head with ideas and beliefs.
>
> I suggest that, on one level, Victoria's Secret is right just where the church has been wrong. More specifically, I think we should first recognize and admit that the marketing industry—which promises an erotically charged transcendence through media that connects to our heart and imagination—is operating with a better, more creational, more incarnational, more holistic anthropology than much of the (evangelical) church.[4]

If we want to be effective preachers, we have to understand how modern marketing works, and we must learn to aim our presentations of Christ's love at the heart as well as the head. We must offer images of God's saving work that stand up against the flashy promises offered in that sexy commercial featuring the shiny new car perched on a desert mesa or the hopes inspired by that carefully staged dream kitchen in the pages of the latest home decorating magazine.

In this chapter I will offer several observations about the way advertisers and image-makers use visual images. Watching how they work will teach us something about how to find and use controlling images in our own communication.

A Strong Image Puts People in a Story

After telling the story of Mabinty Bangura and the image of the ballerina that shaped her life, Virginia Postrel offers this reflection on the potential power of images: "The same imaginative process that led an orphaned child to see her ideal self in a photo of a ballerina has sent nations to war and put men on the moon, transformed the landscape and built business empires."[5] She then goes on to offer an initial explanation of why images have such propulsive power: when we see the images of beautiful models in sports cars or sun-kissed tourists on the beach with a margarita in their hand, "for a moment we project ourselves into the world they represent, a place in which we, too, are beautiful, admired, graceful, courageous, accomplished, desired, powerful, wealthy, or at ease. . . . [Glamour] lifts us out of our everyday experience and makes our desires seem attainable."[6] In other words, when a good image takes hold of our imagination, it puts us in a story. We see the image and we momentarily imagine ourselves transported out of our present lives—with its worries and troubles—and into a more perfect, more joyful, more fulfilling future.

As preachers these sorts of propulsive, story-creating images are just what we want at the center of our sermons. When we preach the gospel we invite our congregations into God's story. We want them to long for the better country of God's kingdom. We want them to be so smitten by the love of God in Jesus Christ our Lord that they are willing to sell everything that they have invested in other stories so that they can possess the pearl of great price. We want the images of the perfect showroom kitchen and airbrushed beauties in lingerie to grow small in their imaginations, replaced by a vivid picture of sacrificial love, Christian joy, and Spirit-filled intimacy.

As we look for controlling images that have that propulsive power, advertisers teach us that not all images are equal in their powers of story creation. In the earlier days of advertising, products were generally not presented with glamorous images that offered the consumer an alternate future; they were presented according to the much smaller world of the product itself. So when a car company tried to sell you a car, it told you that the vehicle would last longer, drive smoother, and get better mileage; the company didn't promise it would change your life. Kevin Roberts, former director of the advertising firm Saatchi & Saatchi, put it this way:

> Products were invented to supply a benefit, a functional attribute to make you feel better. . . . [Advertisements] were based on what I call "ER words": whiter, brighter, cleaner, stronger, fitter. Watch any commercials on American TV and you'll see these words come up in the first three seconds, hammered remorselessly into your brain. But what's happened now is everybody's doing it. Everything works now: French fries taste crisp; coffee's hot; beer tastes good.[7]

In other words, earlier advertising was much more likely to simply show you a picture of the product—here's a can of Maxwell House Coffee—along with words that told you how this product was your best choice (Maxwell

House is good coffee, "good to the last drop"). To use the term I described in the last chapter, most advertising images were merely *denotative*.

But those more prosaic images quickly gave way to an advertising strategy in which products were presented in ways that suggested that a car wasn't just a car and a cup of coffee was more than just a cup of coffee; now they were products that could bring you a whole new life, a whole new future. Advertising became rich in connotative images. Douglas Atkin of the advertising firm Merkley + Partners describes the change:

> There was a time when brands and brand symbols were marks of identification for the producer to say: "This is my product. You can rely on its consistency, the same quality time and time again." Nowadays, producers of brands realize that the consumer needs to say: "No, this is my product, I identify with it. The Apple computer is my computer because it stands for creativity and nonconformism, just like I do," or, "The VW Beetle is my kind of car because it stands for antimaterialism, just like I do."[8]

The product I own tells a story and I want to be part of that story.

Marketers create this storied form of brand allegiance in various ways, but one of the primary tools is the image. For example, in the 1930s, industrial designers and advertisers became infatuated with streamlining. The lines of the new cars (like the Lincoln Zephyr), the shape of the new buildings (like the Chrysler Building), the design of radios and refrigerators all reflected curves and teardrop shapes. Even items like a refrigerator, which were clearly meant to stand still in your kitchen, were given an aerodynamic shape as though they were moving into a glorious future and taking you along with them. The effect was strong enough that New York journalist Joan Kron would sit on the floor with her brother in the 1930s cutting out pictures of these streamlined products: "I was fascinated with car design, these modern cars. Industrial design was very much on our minds. It wasn't just to look at. It was bringing us the future."[9] The streamlined imagery and the futuristic sense it evoked conveyed the promise that science and industry would usher in a brave new world. The pictures touched this young girl's heart and sent her imagination spinning. It put her in a story where technology would save us.

Images that cause us to imagine a future need conscious shaping. "Not just any image, however beautiful or sublime, will do," says Virginia Postrel.

> It requires, therefore, *the creation and transmission of images that invite projection.* These images may be evocative word pictures or visual art, theatrical performances or live glimpses of people, places or artifacts. But

67

whatever the medium, the audience must be able to see themselves in the picture somehow.[10]

When an image achieves this sort of power of projection we sometimes call it *iconic*. Think of the famous image of Che Guevara: the one where his face is upturned, his hair is blowing, and there's a fierceness in his eyes that make him look like he's thinking of revolution. For young Marxists and socialists, for generations of social revolutionaries, that image evokes a whole story of struggle and sacrifice and desire for change. It's still an image that people attach themselves to as an expression of their beliefs (T-shirts! coffee mugs!). It's iconic.

Alberto Korda, Museo Che Guevara, Havana, Cuba

Or think of the stylized campaign poster from Barack Obama's 2008 presidential race where the candidate's face is upturned and the colors of red, white, and blue are overlaid on his image, the word *Hope* written beneath in plain, bold, block letters. For some young Democrats the picture stood for a whole new beginning with a young African American president.[11] It was (and for some still is) iconic.

Or think of the World War II picture of the five Marines planting the American flag at the top of Mount Suribachi on Iwo Jima after a brutal five-week battle that cost thousands of human lives. The five soldiers lean eagerly into their work. The stars and stripes unfurl over the bomb-blasted mountaintop. The image evokes patriotism, sacrifice, determination. It is emblematic of what some have called the Greatest Generation. It is iconic.

So what can advertisers teach preachers about how to make an image iconic rather than simply descriptive? What can they show us about finding good, strong controlling images that propel our sermons? There are at least two lessons we can learn.

Image Should Usually Come Before Explanation

In most television and print advertising, it is pretty clear that advertisers understand that the power of persuasion is in the ad's images, not the text. Words matter, of course. Words, whether text in a print ad or voice-over in a television commercial, give shape and context to an image, but the images do the heavy lifting. Pharmaceutical ads are the clearest example of this.

For example, a 2013 ad for Cialis, a drug designed to help men who deal with erectile dysfunction, features a whole series of compelling images. We are presented with three couples. All of them look like they are about fifty-five years old and all of them are what people call well preserved. The women are thin and vigorous; the men are square-jawed and paunch-free. Most men and women experience lateral spread in middle age, but not these folk.

Couple number one is playing tennis. The wife's long, slender legs are beautifully highlighted by her tennis miniskirt. She hits the ball and he saunters over with a twinkle in his eye. They join hands first and then their arms encircle each other's waist as they walk off the court. The next couple is building a bench together; side by side they apply a finishing coat of lacquer. As they paint he leans closer to her and she looks up with a shy smile. His arm moves to her hip as he gives her a kiss that she warmly receives. The third couple is rowing a boat, sitting side by side together on the bench of the rowboat, each pulling an oar. The sun is getting low in the sky and the water is calm. The woman (who looks about ten years younger than the man) leans toward him and looks at him coyly, finally laying her head on his shoulder. He pulls her close and kisses her on the forehead.

All these images suggest a story. At the most obvious level they suggest the promise of sex. The commercial shows us the first moves of a romantic dance that we all imagine will lead to something a little more robust in the not-too-distant future. At a deeper level, these images promise men and women experiencing the travails of late middle age that they can recapture the fire and virility of their youth; Cialis can bring back the old flame.

The interesting thing about these Cialis commercials (and about all pharmaceutical commercials in the American market) is that while these enticing images present themselves to our imaginations, the commercial's voice-over has a few warnings for us. For fully half of the ad, the announcer cheerfully lists for us a series of horrific side effects, including unsafe drops in blood pressure, headaches, backaches and muscle aches, rashes, hives, swollen lips and tongues, constricting throats, difficult breathing, impaired swallowing, and, of course, the mother of all scary side effects: the erection lasting more than four hours, for which we should seek immediate medical help.

Can we agree that these words have very little persuasive power? Yet still the pharmaceutical companies and the ad agencies they employ continue to sell their product with these commercials full of scary words. They do it because they know that despite the horrendous side effects listed in their disclaimer, the images of middle-aged passion and the promise of restored youth will trump the scary verbiage every time. They've done the research, they've crunched the numbers, and the commercials work because while they cede the valley of reason, they seize the high ground of the imagination. That's how modern advertisers persuade: they lead with the image.

Those of us who have spent a lifetime listening to sermons have actually witnessed a similar phenomenon that also confirms the primacy of image and story. Here's the sermonic equivalent of Cialis commercial: the preacher spends fifteen minutes of his time with explanatory words that are his best attempts to bring his text to his listeners. The words are abstract and flat. The listeners have to work hard to stay with him. But in the middle of all those explanatory words the preacher tells a really powerful story, a story full of luminous detail, one of those stories that causes the whole church to go still, one of those stories where you can feel the congregation listening.

Unfortunately the story is only tangentially connected to the text and the theme of the rest of the sermon, so that if someone asks you a few days later about the sermon, you can recall almost every detail of the story, but you have a terrible time remembering the Bible passage for the day and what the story had to do with it. When a sermon has a story aimed at the imagination that points in a slightly different direction from all the explanatory information in the rest of the sermon, the story (with its visual appeal) sticks while the explanation fades.[12] This is bad. To use the point made in chapter 1, controlling images should be aimed in the same direction as the sermon theme. Unlike a Cialis commercial, preachers should choose images that point in the same direction as the rest of the sermon.

Nevertheless, the way advertisers use images suggests a very particular strategy for the way images and stories should be presented in a sermon. Many times when people use an image, they start by using explanatory language to convey the truth that the image is supposed to represent, so that the image becomes illustrative of the theme. For most preachers the default order is explanation first, image second. Watching the way advertisers structure their communication I would suggest that, homiletically speaking, a better order is story and image first, explanation second.

In addition to what we've already observed, there are a couple of reasons why the image should come before the explanation. First, starting with explanation lets some of the air out of the story and its imagery. When I tell you at the beginning that this story will illustrate the power of forgiving love, in some ways I've already given away the ending. It's a little like prefacing the story of the boy who cried wolf by saying, "Now I'm going to tell you a story that shows how little boys who lie to others won't be believed when it really matters." It doesn't ruin the story but it certainly takes some of the spark out of it. Stories and images engage the imagination best when they are not too obvious, when there is some uncertainty as to how this will all end.

Virginia Postrel tells us that the same principle applies to images used in advertising and popular culture: "A glamorous image appeals to our desires without becoming explicit, lest too much information break the spell. In its blend of accessibility and distance, glamour is neither transparent nor opaque. It is translucent."[13] When images and stories are explained before they are revealed, they leave a much shallower impression in the imagination of the hearer.

Second, putting the image and story before the explanation fits the optimal learning pattern described by both Jamie Smith and Robert Frost in the previous chapter. Frost said that the best poems travel a path from delight to wisdom. The poem begins with delighted sight: an image of something in the world that catches attention. The poet then moves to a luminous description of what he or she has seen; he or she paints the picture. And then, only after the vision has been seen and carefully illumined, does the poet make the move to wisdom, offering a reflection on what the image might say about life.

Jamie Smith suggested that this delight-to-wisdom pattern doesn't just describe a good poem, it describes the path that all our learning and thinking follows: "Because we are affective before we are cognitive (and even while we are cognitive), visions of the good get inscribed in us by means that are commensurate with our primarily affective, imaginative nature." And in Smith's account, the means by which these visions of the good life are inscribed are "stories, legends, myths, plays, novels and films rather than dissertations, messages and monographs."[14] The stories and the images come first, the cognition follows.

If Smith and Frost are right in their descriptions of human thinking (and I think they are), then the default order for our presentation of material in sermons should be image first, explanation second.

That doesn't mean there should never be any introduction to stories or that controlling images should just appear out of the blue. Good storytellers know that a few words of introduction can shape the way the listener hears the story without giving away the ending. And there are times when a preacher will choose to tell a story as an illustration that follows a concept that he's presented. Nevertheless, the default mode should be: image first, explanation second.

A Good Image Must Be Properly Framed

Earlier I used the example of Che Guevara's portrait as an image that had propulsive power. For millions of young Marxists and socialists, Che's fierce look represented their determination to fulfill the ideals of the revolution and build a better world. This iconic photograph would never have had that sort of power if it hadn't been carefully framed.

The image was taken in 1960 by Alberto Korda at a funeral for the victims of a Belgian arms freighter that had exploded in the Havana harbor. Korda was photographing people at the funeral, and when Guevara appeared, Korda snapped a couple of shots. Here is the original image as it appeared on Korda's roll of film.

Alberto Korda, Museo Che Guevara, Havana, Cuba

It's a good picture, but with the tree and the profile of the other man in the frame, it looks less like an iconic image of the revolution and more like the picture of a man at a funeral, lost in his thoughts. The other objects in the frame make the image less iconic, less universally applicable, and more tied to a specific time and place.

But now look what happens when Korda reframes the image.

The tree is gone and so is the other funeral guest. Most of Guevara's leather jacket is cropped so that his face is accented. When Guevara is isolated from his surroundings and presented as a solitary figure, he is no longer a man at a funeral; now he is a man alone facing life and its fears. Because he is alone and the context has been removed, it becomes much easier for us to identify with him and imagine that we share his context. Furthermore, because the background detail is removed and his face is central, we have a stronger sense that the expression on Guevara's face is one of determination and revolu-

Alberto Korda, Museo Che Guevara, Havana, Cuba

tionary vision, rather than distracted grief. The framing turns an ordinary image into something iconic.[15]

Chip and Dan Heath know the importance of framing. In *Made to Stick* they tell the story of two different letters sent out by Save the Children, a charity that focuses on the well-being of children all over the world. Both letters solicited donations from the recipients, but each letter framed the appeal differently.

The first letter made its appeal with broad statistics about the challenges that face children in the developing world: "More than 11 million people in Ethiopia need immediate food assistance. Food shortages in Malawi are affecting more than three million people."[16] The first letter had a wide-angle focal length, showing as many needy folks as possible.

The second letter went in for a close-up. This letter gave the story of one needy seven-year-old in Mali named Rokia and told recipients very specifically how their donations would help her. Instead of focusing on the millions, the camera zoomed in on a single story. The frame was trimmed and the image was simpler and more evocative. The people who read the second letter gave twice as much as those who received the first one.[17]

A good example of this sort of framing can be seen in Frederick Buechner's sermon, "The Magnificent Defeat." In this sermon Buechner explores the character of Jacob as presented to us in Genesis, and Buechner quite rightly observes that Jacob is a schemer. Genesis shows us a man who grabs and pushes his way through life, determined to make it by the power of his own substantial cleverness. For years it works for him, until one night when he comes to the ford of the Jabbok River to meet his estranged brother. At that moment, Jacob knows that all his ill-begotten chickens are coming home to roost, and he is in a state of panic. That night he meets a stranger down by the river and, true to his scheming character, he tries to wrestle the stranger into submission, just as he has spent his days trying to wrestle his whole life into submission.

Buechner frames the scene by showing how at first Jacob seems to be winning. His scheming seems to be working. Then his opponent reaches out and touches him on the hip and suddenly Jacob is sinking. He holds on tightly to his opponent; only now he grabs at his opponent like a drowning man in full panic. He cries out for a blessing from his foe because he finally realizes that what he needs can't be won through scheming and grabbing; it can only be received as a gift.

Then, in a brilliant bit of framing, Buechner widens the frame to our lives, and suddenly we are the ones wrestling and scheming, and our opponent is Christ.

> Power, success, happiness, as the world knows them, are his who will fight for them hard enough; but peace, love, joy, are only from God. And God is the enemy whom Jacob fought there by the river, of course, and whom in one way or another we all of us fight—God, the beloved enemy. Our enemy because, before giving us everything, he demands of us everything; before giving us life, he demands our lives our selves, our wills, our treasure.
>
> Will we give them, you and I? I do not know. Only remember the last glimpse that we have of Jacob, limping home against the great conflagration of the dawn. Remember Jesus of Nazareth, staggering on broken feet out of the tomb toward the Resurrection, bearing on his body the proud insignia of the defeat which is victory, the magnificent defeat of the human soul at the hands of God.[18]

This is the end of the sermon, and once again it is beautifully framed. You can read the story of Jacob wrestling God at the ford of the Jabbok simply as an important event in the life of one man. You can read it as something that happened to Jacob alone, an event only tangentially related to us and our struggles.

But by emphasizing several details, Buechner changes everything. First he describes the struggle of Jacob to take control of his life in terms that resonate with our own struggle for mastery: "God is the enemy whom Jacob fought there by the river, of course, whom in one way or another we all of us fight—God the beloved enemy." The story is framed in such a way that Jacob's nighttime contest is also our dark night of the soul.

And more importantly, when Jacob finally surrenders, Buechner takes the picture of Jacob crossing the river the next morning, an image that is in the biblical text ("The sun rose upon him as Jacob passed Penuel, limping because of his thigh," Gen 32:31), and he makes it resonate with Easter morning when Jesus limped out of the tomb having wrestled death to the ground and pinned it on our behalf. In a single image we suddenly see the overwhelming grace of God. In a single image we see that our hope lies not in strength and control but in the rising sun of God's mercy. The frame makes the image work.

There are lessons to be learned here. Fashion designers, graphic artists, and advertising executives are not typical company for preachers. But they have worked long and hard to understand how images work on the human heart, and they have exercised enormous creative energy in crafting images that persuade. Whether or not these artists acknowledge the one who shaped the heart and formed the imagination, they have been perceptive observers of the warp and the woof of the imagination as God formed it when knitting us together in our mothers' wombs. A little time sitting at their feet is time well spent.

How to Find
a Controlling Image

By now you may be convinced that good sermons are centered on one controlling image or phrase. You may also agree that a poet can use a single image to propel the reader into a wider world of deeper meaning. But even at this point, a serious problem may remain. How do you find a good image? How do you select an appropriate, effective centering phrase? Anyone who has ever tried to preach knows that this does not happen automatically. It's all very well to talk about the importance of controlling images and phrases, but how in heaven's name do you find one?

Poet David Citino talks about prolonged spells of "hemming and hawing."[1] Barbara Brown Taylor talks about running the rod of God's word over our experience.[2] Thornton Wilder talks about the key line of a sonnet dropping from the ceiling like a gift and the poet tapping away at it with a jeweler's hammer.[3] These are wonderful descriptions, but they hardly add up to a disciplined approach. What can we do to find our image Sunday after Sunday? The one line of the sonnet may drop down to the writer from the ceiling, but surely the writer can do more than stare at the ceiling and wait for its appearance.

Although I have done my fair share of ceiling watching over the years, I believe we can do more. And there are people who can help us. For example, poets can be our teachers here. After years of lion taming and alligator wrestling, writers have learned a thing or two about making poems happen. Novelists, essayists, English professors, and poets have all weighed in on this subject, all of them offering various suggestions about how to improve their work, some of them dealing specifically with the quest for the controlling image.

But some teachers are closer to home. In the ranks of those who practice traditional Christian disciplines, we find many men and women who've thought about letting faith rule the imagination of the heart. These people have developed practices designed to open themselves up, readying themselves to receive images and phrases given by the Spirit through the word.

In this chapter I will review some how-to suggestions from people who've thought about finding images that speak to the heart. Most of the wisdom we'll learn will come from the world of poetry, but I will also spend time reviewing the Christian practice of *lectio divina*, or sacred reading. It's a little different from the disciplines practiced by poets, but it shows us a way of coming to scripture with our hearts open and our imaginations attuned. By the end of the chapter we will have some very concrete suggestions of things we might do to find controlling images for our sermons.

Looking for a Controlling Image:
Lectio Divina

The quest for a controlling image is a different sort of quest. When a preacher picks up his exegetical tools and begins his search for a biblical theme, he follows a well-traveled path. Generations of seminarians have had the steps of exegesis drilled into their heads: take your text, our professors told us, analyze the languages, study the literary and historical context of those texts, read your commentaries, examine the keywords, pay attention to the wisdom of the great theologians of the past, and you'll have a pretty good idea of what the text is about. Follow these directions and you will be able to formulate the text's theme. Seminary-trained preachers know how to follow this map.

Following the exegetical path is critical to good biblical preaching. Whatever a preacher says in the sermon must be governed by the message of the biblical text, and once mastered, these familiar directions help ministers discern that message skillfully and make it easy for them to write down their themes.

But the kind of reading and studying an exegete does is only one kind of reading. In their first year of study, seminarians who go to a traditional, exegetically focused school will have an experience something like this: Seminarians will spend all day studying the Bible. In their Old Testament class the students will read (for example) Genesis 1, and it will be the most detailed reading they have ever experienced. The professor will uncover both the similarities and differences between the Genesis narrative and the other creation stories of the ancient Near East. The students will learn the names Marduk and Tiamat, and when they compare the stories of these Babylonian gods to the story of Genesis 1 they will have all sorts of insights into the text's history and meaning.

Then in the Gospels class students will hear a lecture on the synoptic problem: Why do the gospels seem to differ so sharply in the details of many of their stories? The professor will show students differences between Matthew and Luke that they'd never noticed before. The professor will tell them that most scholars think Luke and Matthew were written with the book of Mark sitting open on the table, and the professor will teach the students why scholars believe that the other synoptic authors used it. On top of all this, the professor will also introduce the Q hypothesis. It's a packed class!

In systematic theology class they will talk about eschatology and the difference between premillennial and amillennial traditions. Part of the discussion will review the theological positions of both camps, but most of the discussion will refer to texts in Thessalonians and Revelation and Daniel, talking about the different ways people interpret those passages.

Finally in social ethics class seminarians will study the boundary line between religion and politics. While much of the discussion involves analysis of the way church and state have related to one another throughout history, the professor will also refer constantly to Bible texts that speak to the issue, texts such as Romans 13, Revelation 13, and Mark 12:13-17.

All day long seminarians are immersed in scripture. And yet, at the end of the day, the student will feel like something is missing. The student will feel a hunger to pick up his Bible and read it. But this time it's not a learned grammatical or historical reading that the seminarian wants; this time, instead of reading the Bible in analytical mode, the student wants to read scripture in a posture of surrendered attention. This time the budding scholar wants a devotional reading.

The seminary classroom training I've described is wonderful. There is startling depth in scripture and plumbing those depths is a great adventure. And yet, from its earliest days, the church has identified another kind of reading, devotional reading, and the church has said that this kind of reading is an essential formative practice for believers. After a long day in the classroom, when a young seminarian finds himself strangely hungry for the Bible, it's a devotional reading he wants.

One style of devotional reading that has some ancient roots but also enjoys modern popularity is the practice of *lectio divina*. In the last thirty years many very well educated pastors and laypeople have turned to *lectio* as a practice that can satisfy the need for a more devotional reading. Maybe because it is a more devotional kind of reading,[4] not only can *lectio* fill a desire for a more personal approach to the word, but it can also be a way in which, led by the Spirit, we might find images and phrases to anchor our sermons.

The Steps of Lectio Divina

Preparation: Get yourself to a place where distractions will be minimal and where you will be able to sit comfortably for at least fifteen minutes. "Spend the first few minutes getting physically quiet and spiritually centered."[5] Many guides suggest paying attention to your breathing as a way to find a quiet center.

Reading: Choose a short unit of scripture—one story, one psalm, one parable, one prophecy—and read it out loud. Don't just read the text once; read it multiple times and as you read, listen for a personal word. As one specialist puts it: "Savor each portion of the reading, constantly listening for the 'still, small voice' of a word or phrase that somehow says, 'I am for you today.'"[6] If your passage is a narrative, imagine yourself there in that place. Imagine what's happening around you as the story unfolds.

Meditation: Out of the longer reading, focus on a phrase, a word, or an image that has been given to you, and ruminate on it. Michael Quicke calls this the stage that "enables a preacher to enter more fully into a text, to visualize its story, to dwell in its words and images, to open up all the senses to God's action in it."[7] When it comes to finding a controlling image, this might be the most fruitful stage of *lectio*, focused as it is on visual. Other spiritual writers favor metaphors of mastication when they describe this stage of the process: "This chewing of the word, savoring it and leisurely dwelling with it, requires becoming very familiar with the word. Often this is done by focusing on an image, a phrase or even one word from a text at a time."[8] Let this image or phrase speak to your life and its worries and fears, its joys and hopes.

Contemplation: End the session with a time of prayer. This prayer could simply be a time of resting in the presence of God, grateful for the word the Spirit has given. It is also a time where you simply respond to God, to the word or the image God has given, and ask God to remake your life in light of that word.

These steps are not rigid—different *lectio* experts offer slight variations on how to approach the practice—but the overall ethos of contemplation, openness, and imaginative engagement is common to all the approaches.

In their book *Discovering* Lectio Divina, James Wilhoit and Evan Howard don't just outline the *lectio* process, they also describe an individual session and the thoughts and feelings that it evoked. Not only is this account helpful in teaching a reader how to practice *lectio divina*, but also for our purposes it shows how it can lift up strong images.

One of the authors (the book doesn't say which one) practices *lectio* with Luke 5:17-26, the story where Jesus heals the paralytic who was lowered through the roof of the home where Jesus was preaching.[9] The author composes himself and begins his session by reading the passage out loud, letting each phrase speak to him.

The passage begins: "One day when Jesus was teaching, Pharisees and legal experts were sitting nearby. They had come from every village in Galilee and Judea, and from Jerusalem. Now the power of the Lord was with Jesus to heal" (v. 17). That concluding phrase strikes him. "I stop. I think a little. What does it mean 'the power of the Lord was with him to heal'? Wasn't the power of God always with Jesus? I decide I can't solve this."[10]

The author continues his meditative reading. He reads slowly, phrase by phrase through the section where the friends of the paralytic bring the man to Jesus and, to avoid the crowds, climb onto the roof and lower him down. He writes: "As I read this section, I picture the scene: the building, the men carrying the bed with the paralytic, the crowd. I identify with the frustration of those men carrying the bed and their inability to get through the crowd."[11] He starts thinking about roofs in those days and how much noise it must have made to make the hole and lower the man.

None of the reflection so far is really grabbing his imagination, so his mind starts to wander. He starts thinking about his sister, remembering that he needed to write her on Facebook and wish her a happy birthday. These sorts of distractions are typical, and he shakes it off by continuing to read.

The passage moves to the point where Jesus first sees the man and responds by saying, "Friend, your sins are forgiven," which causes the Pharisees to grumble, "Only God can forgive sins!" (vv. 20-21). As the author imagines the scene his mind starts to move in a more personal direction: "I remember last year. What I did last year was stupid. I know it was wrong. Some people at work still haven't forgiven me."[12]

He begins to think about Jesus forgiving the paralytic and then he reads how Jesus healed the man by saying, "I say to you, get up, take your cot, and go home" (v. 24). He thinks, "I've been paralyzed ever since that event. I just can't seem to move forward or stand up. I wish I could stand up. I'm here, God. How does this forgiveness and healing thing work?" All of a sudden the author hears the words that Jesus spoke to the paralytic again, only this time they're not spoken to the first-century man on the mat but to the twenty-first-century man looking for forgiveness. "I feel him calling me 'friend.' For a few moments my distractions are gone, and I am there facing Jesus who looks at me and tells me my sins are forgiven."[13]

As the author finishes reading the passage, he sees the description of the former paralytic glorifying and praising God as he carries his mat homeward. All day long he allows this image of Christ's forgiveness to permeate him and he resolves to stand up straight and go through his day praising God, just like the paralytic. Throughout the day the image of Jesus calling him "friend," forgiving him, and calling him to stand up straight returns to his imagination, giving him strength and joy for his work. The text fills his heart and shapes his day.

Of course, not all *lectio divina* sessions are this fruitful, but as we watch the process described by Wilhoit and Howard, we get a good sense of how productive the exercise can be, how it might well generate the kind of controlling images that would ground a message. In this case that picture of the man receiving forgiveness and then standing up straight is a specific picture that could carry a whole sermon. As I think about it, it strikes me how guilt and shame are like a crippling weight, how we actually talk about people "crushed by guilt" and "bent down with shame." The picture in this story embodies the truth that forgiveness allows broken people to stand and go forward with joy.

There are caveats here. Wilhoit and Howard acknowledge them. After the session the author reflects on whether or not his picture of forgiveness and standing up straight, the picture he received as a personal word, is actually in line with the theme of the text as a grammatical and historical exegete might describe it. Would his devotional reading line up with a careful analytic reading?

Most exegetes would say that this text is about Jesus demonstrating that he is the Son of God. Both in his forgiveness of sins and in his healing, Jesus gives a sign that he is the Messiah. Does the image fit that broader theme?

I think it does. It's because Jesus is actually the Son of God that we can rely on his forgiveness. It's because Jesus is actually the Son of God that we can know he has the power to make us stand up straight. After all, aren't the two moments of his miracle, the forgiveness followed by the healing, repeated later in Jesus's great saving work on the weekend of his Passion? Wasn't that weekend an offering of forgiveness (the cross) followed by a healing (the resurrection)? Aren't the death and resurrection of Jesus the reasons we are all forgiven, healed, called to stand up straight, and sent on our way rejoicing?

Maybe this connection convinces you, maybe it doesn't. Either way, the caveat here is the same caveat that we've repeated throughout this book: your image must match the exegetical theme of your passage. If the image doesn't fit the theme of the text, it won't work in a sermon.

Looking at the process as a whole, I am enthusiastic about *lectio divina* as a spiritual practice that can help us read texts differently. When done faithfully and prayerfully, it's a practice that the Spirit can use to open up the visual side of the text and help us find controlling images for our sermons.

Looking for a Controlling Image: Poetic Exercises

Although they generally work in what would be considered a secular milieu, poets often look for controlling images to anchor their work, and just like preachers, they know that the search involves a different sort of process than one finds in the world of exegesis or scholarly inquiry. Robert Frost summarizes the differences by saying, "scholars get their [knowledge] with conscientious thoroughness along projected lines of logic," while poets get their knowledge "cavalierly." They walk through the fields of life and material sticks to them "like burrs."[14]

Perhaps wandering through fields and hoping burrs stick to you isn't a promising metaphor for preachers facing the very regular pressure of Sunday morning. When we're hunched over our computers on a Friday eager to finish our sermons, we feel rather pressed for time and waiting for burrs to stick is a luxury we can't afford. But while there are no guaranteed "Follow my method and you'll get an image every time" processes out there in the world of creative writing, there are at least some disciplines, some habits of vision we preachers might adopt to help the burrs stick. Let's listen to what the poets have to teach us.

Learning to See the Details

In chapter 3 we saw that specific details are important to a poem; almost universally, when poets give suggestions for writing good poetry, they tell aspiring writers to cultivate a keen eye for detail. You must learn to see, they tell us.

Poet Linda Gregg gives her students an exercise designed to make that happen. She tells her students to take a close look at six things every day.[15] Such focused attention takes discipline. Most of us slide through the world without noticing the small details. We are habitually unobservant, and we have to force ourselves to look carefully. Even published poets have to work at this, says Ted Kooser. But when we do force ourselves to look, imaginative doors open.

Kooser followed Gregg's exercise by taking a poetic expedition to the mall. Notebook in hand, he sat in the midst of the bustle, determined to observe more carefully the details of that place. The result was "Cosmetics Department," a poem that came from his close observation of the women who sit behind the cosmetic counters at the upscale stores, surrounded by the tools of the cosmetic trade and offering to help any person who will sit on their stool. He pictures them as sorceresses in black capes performing an age-defying magic.

The poem shows us two young women sitting at the counter, one who works there and applies the makeup, the other a customer getting a makeover. But through the poet's imagination this sight, common to any mall-goer, is transformed into an occult ritual in which a sorceress gives her subject the gift of eternal youth but does so at the expense of her humanity. Kooser calls their faces "cool" and "white" and "frozen forever," and the lines between the cosmetics counter and the mortuary are suddenly blurred. Like the dead, their faces give off a "cool light."[16]

The exercise seems to have worked. I think this is an effective poem that does more than describe what you see at the mall; it causes us to reflect on larger questions of death and beauty. The observation exercise has yielded a strong image and an evocative poem.

Preachers can easily adapt this exercise. As part of your sermon preparation, you could take a biblical text and write down all the objects (or images) of the text. This should include more than inanimate objects, it should also identify scenes—moments that can be pictured as snapshots.

Let's take a particular biblical text and see how this exercise might work. Let's make an image list based on Psalm 77. The psalm will be on the left and the images that appear in the psalm will appear in the right column beside the verse in which they appear.

1 I cry out loud to God—   *Image: a cry for help*
   out loud to God so that he can hear me!
2 During the day when I'm in trouble I look for my Lord.
   At night my hands are still outstretched and don't grow numb;
     my whole being refuses to be
      comforted.   *Image: outstretched hands*
3 I remember God and I moan.   *Image: groaning psalmist*
   I complain, and my spirit grows tired.

4 You've kept my eyelids from closing.   *Image: sleeplessness*
   I'm so upset I can't even speak.
5 I think about days long past;
   I remember years that seem an eternity in the past.
6 I meditate with my heart at night;   *Image: singing in the darkness*
   I complain, and my spirit keeps searching:
7 "Will my Lord reject me forever?
   Will he never be pleased again?
8 Has his faithful love come to a complete end?
   Is his promise over for future generations?
9 Has God forgotten how to be gracious?
   Has he angrily stopped up his compassion?"
10 It's my misfortune, I thought,
   that the strong hand of the Most High is
     different now.   *Image: the right hand of the Lord*

11 But I will remember the LORD's deeds;
   yes, I will remember your wondrous acts from times long past.
12 I will meditate on all your works;
   I will ponder your deeds.
13 God, your way is holiness!
   Who is as great a god as you, God?
14 You are the God who works wonders;
   you have demonstrated your strength among all peoples.
15 With your mighty arm you redeemed your people;
   redeemed the children of Jacob and Joseph.

16 The waters saw you, God— the waters saw you
   and reeled!   *Image: churning waters*
 Even the depths shook!
17 The clouds poured water, the skies cracked
   thunder;   *Image: a thunderstorm downpour*

your arrows were flying all
around!   *Image: lightning as God's arrows*
18 The crash of your thunder was in the swirling storm;
lightning lit up the whole world;
the earth shook and quaked.
19 Your way went straight through the sea;   *Image: a path through*
your pathways went right through the mighty waters.
But your footprints left no trace!   *Image: unseen footprints*
20 You led your people like sheep under the care of Moses and Aaron.
Image: the hands of Moses and Aaron

This isn't the most visual of psalms, and yet we've already found twelve solid images with which to work. I'm sure a careful reader could find still more. But even these twelve images, gathered in ten minutes, are sufficient to stir the imagination. For example, I like the play of hand imagery in this psalm: the outstretched hand of the psalmist leads to the strong right hand of God, which in turn displays itself through the hands of Moses and Aaron. This is an image that could suggest both the trouble and the grace of the sermon: the trouble might be pictured by the psalmist's hand reaching out in pain in the middle of the night, while the grace of the sermon could be captured by the strong right hand of the Lord reaching out to help the psalmist, a hand that often manifests itself through the human hands like the hands of Moses and Aaron.

Another image possibility presents itself in the unseen footprints of verse 19. The psalmist is obviously frustrated because he is in some sort of trouble. Waves of trouble foam around him and he can't find God in his storm. But when he thinks back to the past deliverance of God's people he remembers how, in the miracle of the Red Sea, even though God was completely present and acted mightily, God's footprints were unseen. The image reminds us how the presence and grace of God are always partly hidden, how the direct action of God can be as hard to trace as footprints on water.

Or maybe a different image strikes you; that's fine. Either way this poetic exercise applied to preaching does help us find a controlling image for our sermon.[17]

The Three Levels of an Image: Senses, Feeling, and Thought

Here's another exercise to help you see. This one not only gets you to notice details, but it also helps you work with them.

Kooser and Cox suggest that if a writer wants to jump-start his or her work, he or she might try a systematic examination of *input*.[18] What is a writer's input? It's simply the image he or she is writing about. I know that telling you to examine the image you're writing about seems obvious and dull, but I think you will find this exercise fruitful.

Kooser and Cox break down input into three distinct parts: sensations, feelings, and thoughts. Here's how that breakdown looks. Suppose the item you're looking at (your input) is a wilted rose in your mother's garden.

1. First, you describe the rose as it presents itself to your *senses*. You include descriptions of how it looks, how the flowers around it look, how it smells, and so on. That's the sense level of input.

2. Next comes the level of *feeling*. How does this rose make you feel? When you look at it carefully, what emotions does it evoke? Do you feel sadness over the ending of beauty? Do you feel loss because your mother's gardening abilities are in decline? Do you feel guilt because you were supposed to water the roses while your mom was on vacation but somehow you managed to forget? What emotions are attached to this wilted rose?

3. Finally there is the level of *thought*. "What do you think about what you felt and saw?"[19] Here's where your focus on one thing begins to widen into a reflection on something universal. Maybe this wilted rose—and here I'm being somewhat schmaltzy—makes you think of all sorts of ways in which we neglect our best relationships and take their beauty for granted.

Do you see what happened to your rose? You've taken one sense impression in your hands like a piece of clay, and, like a craftsman, you've worked it into a useful form. You've given it depth and dimension. You've made it an image that might center a poem or a short essay. Notice, too, that the stages of Kooser and Cox's input examination (from sense to emotion to thought) follows the delight-to-wisdom trajectory Robert Frost ascribed to good poetry, a trajectory I reviewed more thoroughly in chapter 3. You begin with the delight of the rose's sensory description; you end up with the wisdom of your thoughts on the wilted rose.

How might these three levels of input work for a preacher trying to find his or her center amid the beautiful mess? Let's try it out on a biblical text and see.

Let's take Genesis 4:1-15, the story of Cain's murder of Abel and his subsequent banishment from the land. What would happen if we took a couple of details from the text and examined them using Cox and Kooser's three levels of input?

For starters, we could look at Abel's blood crying out from the ground. On the first level, the level of the senses, we can imagine the red stain spreading out from Abel's broken body. We can see the red sharp against the green grass of the field. On a sensory level maybe it reminds us of those pictures of a Baghdad marketplace shattered by a suicide bomber where, even after the bodies have been taken away, the blood pools in the dust as testimony to what happened there.

On the second level of input, the level of feeling, we sense horror at the loss of innocent life. We feel outrage at the injustice. What is Abel's blood crying? What word does the blood speak? Is it saying, "Revenge!"? Is it a word of sorrow and lament? Is it a word of accusation? Is the blood asking for help? What is the blood saying? I imagine the blood crying out some wild mix of anger, sorrow, and impatience.

Now the third level, the level of thought: What do we make of this crying blood? I wonder if all the animal sacrifices of the Old Testament weren't attempts to keep the blood from crying too loudly, to keep that fearful voice from frightening us. I wonder what sort of modern practices are designed to silence the blood (drugs, alcohol, shopping, reality TV, ESPN). Hebrews 12:24 says that the blood of Jesus "speaks better than Abel's blood"—what is the blood of Jesus saying?

This is a fruitful exercise; we have an image around which we can build a sermon. It's not the only image in this text we could have examined with senses, feeling, and thought. Any image or phrase in a text that captures either the trouble or the grace in a text would be a candidate for this sort of input analysis, and there are several of those in Genesis 4:1-15. The image of Cain angry and resentful (or as other translations have it: "with his face downcast") is potent, capturing the trouble of this text. So is the image of the land of Nod, the place of Cain's mournful exile. On the grace side there is the mark of Cain, which protects this sinner in his exile. I also think the image of God asking Cain to master his sin so it won't possess him (Gen 4:7) is an image that points to God's gracious mastery of sin through the sacrifice of Jesus when humankind proved unable to conquer sin on its own. Any phrase or sharp image that might capture the grace or the trouble of a biblical text is a good candidate for input analysis. Take a central image, examine it carefully at the level of sense and feeling and thought, and you may find yourself with a center for your sermon.

Matching the Image to the Theme

I have suggested that a good sermon ought to have a clearly identified governing image as well as a clearly stated sermonic theme. Both are equally important, the theme centering the exegetical study (what Craddock called the hard-chair study) and the image centering the craft side of the sermon (what Craddock calls the soft-chair study). Furthermore I've said that the theme and the image should be related and that they should work in harmony. Given all that, one of the challenges in sermon preparation is making sure your theme and your image work together. Your controlling image needs to open up your theme and help accomplish your sermon's goal; if it doesn't the sermon will tear in two.

Poets Roger Mitchell and Carol Muske have a couple of exercises that might help us match theme and image. Mitchell gives his students famous maxims from ancient philosophers and then makes them write a poem using one of these sayings as an epigraph.[20] The sayings are things like: "The path up and down is one and the same," Heraclitus; "Worlds are altered rather than destroyed," Democritus; "All things were together. Then the mind came and arranged them," Anaxagoras; "[Parmenides] speaks of perceiving and thinking as the same thing," Theophrastus. All of these epigraphs are interesting, and more important for our purposes, they all look a little like theme sentences. Mitchell is teaching students to propel a theme using poetic, imagistic language.

His students must take these abstract ideas and work them into poems by showing what they're trying to tell; in other words they must tell the truth of the saying by showing the reader some concrete detail. Mitchell wants to add a qualification to the "show, don't tell" mantra of all writers. He suggests that all writers try to tell something when they write; no one[21] is engaged in pure showing. Real poets try to use concrete "show" language to tell the reader something: "'show don't tell' sounds like 'don't ever tell' or 'telling is bad.' The truth is, we all want to tell. It is natural to want to tell. Why else write except to tell?"[22]

Mitchell wants to change the mantra to "tell by showing,"[23] which, when you think about it, is what preachers try to do every week. Mitchell's exercise trains his students to turn a theme into an imaginative work. Preachers might devote some of their preparation time to doing what he says, even trying to write a few lines of poetry to free them from excessively linear or abstract thought.

Carol Muske's exercise is also directly helpful in actually making the move from abstract to concrete. She gives her students an abstract word—words such as love, death, justice, joy—and then she asks her students to write down what they "saw" when she spoke the word. This is her way of showing students that "the mind does not 'think' in abstractions." So, for example, when she offers the word "love," her students come back with images like "hearts, a loved one's face," or the color red. One time she did the exercise with first-graders. She gave them the word *happiness* and one little girl told her, "I feel like a big orange sun is coming up inside my body."[24] That's good stuff. That will preach.

A hybrid of these two exercises might work well for preachers trying to come up with a good image to go along with their sermon theme. Take your sermon theme and make a list of images that come up in association with it. First choose images that come from inside the text, then move on to any images that might come to you from outside the text.

Let's practice this with a specific text and a specific theme. While I will work here with my own text, you might take a text you are going to preach and do a parallel exercise, using mine as a kind of template.

Step 1. Choose a theme. In chapter 1 when we were discussing sermon themes and their limitations we noted that Sid Greidanus suggests a sermon theme[25] for John 13:12-17: "Followers of Christ ought to render humble service to one another."[26]

Step 2. Associate the theme with biblical images. Let's take that theme and say what we associate with it. John 13 tells the story of Jesus washing his disciples' feet. Here are some images from the text that show what Jesus tells in verses 12-17:

A cracked foot, worn from journeys into all sorts of places, good and bad.
Jesus stripped of his outer clothing with a towel around his waist.
Jesus kneeling before Judas.
Jesus pouring the water into the bowl.
Jesus untying the thongs of the disciple's sandals.

All of these images are vivid and specific, and they powerfully show humility and service. That makes them great candidates for controlling images that would work closely with the sermon's theme. I like the last image, especially when I compare it to John 1:27 (where John the Baptist said, "He comes after me, but I'm not worthy to untie his sandal straps"). This image gives you so much more grist for the sermonic mill compared to the rather bare "Followers of Christ ought to render humble service to each other."

Step 3. Identify images from experience. Does this theme suggest any images outside the text? Here are some that occur to me:

> Henri Nouwen caring for Adam, the profoundly disabled adult
>
> A bubbling spring in the center of a village that gives itself every day for the cleansing, the feeding, the life of the people
>
> A beast of burden doing its work quietly and faithfully
>
> Sam Gamgee from *The Lord of the Rings*

These are interesting, too, although, as we have previously discussed, probably not as strong as images from inside the text. Still, with the right kind of development, any of these could be a centering image for a sermon on this text.

Imagining a Hearer

A further important step in developing a controlling image for preaching is to imagine a hearer (or reader). This helps in the overall process of making the image specific. In their book *Writing Brave and Free*, Ted Kooser and Steve Cox make some suggestions for helping young writers get started. One of their suggestions is, "When you begin to write, have a reader in mind." What does writing for a specific reader do? It helps focus your thoughts. "Having a reader in mind means finding common ground with your reader. It helps you choose what—of the ten thousand people, places, thoughts, and feelings you know—to write about for that reader."[27]

The beginning writer faces the same problem as the preacher; an explosion of words and images and occurrences is out there in the world, all of it legitimate material for a poem or book. But the poet can't write about all of it; the poet must choose, and one of the ways to choose is to imagine a particular reader in a particular set of circumstances, and let that focus the writing.

Cox and Kooser use the example of a memoir written by Nora Foster describing her experiences after the American Civil War. Foster was born in 1858 in rural Iowa and obviously she had a rich storehouse of scattered impressions and disparate memories from her childhood, all of which could have made it into her book. This jumble of remembrances found order when Foster imagined a reader. She addressed her book to her two grandchildren. She wrote at their level and assumed their life experience as she communicated. As a result her jumbled experiences gained focus and power.[28]

Something similar happened with a children's book on Psalm 23 (NIV) illustrated by Tim Ladwig. Ladwig takes this familiar psalm with its myriad associations, and he imagines a specific reader for it. In this case he imagines two African American children living in the urban core of a twentieth-century American city. By imagining these two children as his readers, Ladwig brings the kind of focus to the psalm that preachers look for every week. When the psalm says, "I shall not want," Ladwig pictures the kids having breakfast in the morning. When the psalmist says, "Even though I walk through the valley of the shadow of death," Ladwig pictures the children walking to school through the canyon of graffiti-covered, boarded-up buildings in the city's core. When the psalmist says, "You prepare a table for me," Ladwig pictures the family sitting down for an evening dinner even while outside their door the neighborhood is filled with sirens and trouble. When the psalmist says, "You anoint my head with oil and my cup overflows," Ladwig pictures one of the children sitting in the bathtub, laughing while he pours water over his head from a cup.[29]

Tim Ladwig is not a poet; he's not even a writer; he's an artist. But his approach to this particular book illustrates how an artist reframes things to create meaning. The artist finds a unique angle of vision and so reveals unseen meaning in familiar objects and texts. Ladwig finds his angle, he finds his frame, and he generates his controlling image by imagining a reader.

How might this insight be applied to the preacher as he or she approaches the text for Sunday morning? How might preachers imagine a hearer? Here's a simple suggestion: as you read the text, imagine different people listening to this scripture with you. Imagine a twelve-year-old middle-school child whose biggest worries are pimples and popularity: How would the text comfort and challenge this child? Imagine a person undergoing chemotherapy: How would this person hear it? What about burned-out teachers, high-powered lawyers who look like they're on top of the world, a single mother trying to hold her family together, a lonely resident in a nursing home? These imaginary people are all types, of course. The exercise works best if you can imagine specific people with real problems in concrete situations. Putting yourself in a specific listener's shoes can make certain parts of the text leap out at you, it can bring certain gracious promises to the surface; it can stimulate new questions. These promises and problems can then become the center of the sermon; they can provide you with your angle, your frame.

This exercise is especially useful with a certain kind of text. If the *Sitz im Leben* of the Bible passage in question is not immediately clear, or if it is altogether unknown, picturing a listener becomes extremely useful. Most of the Psalms work well with this kind of exercise. Scholars have some idea of the original situation in which psalms were written and used, but in most cases the original setting for any psalm is far from certain.

Psalm 16, for example, is clearly a celebration of God's faithfulness in the life of a person who is surveying the course of his (or her?) life. It's a positive poem that elicits a generally warm response from those who hear it. But the psalm gets more traction in imagination and memory when you imagine it in a specific setting. For instance, I know an elderly woman who chose this psalm as the reading for her funeral. She had raised three children on her own after her minister husband died of a heart attack when she was in her thirties. She never remarried, choosing instead to raise her children on her own. So now imagine this: a single mom, strapped for cash, every second of her life spent working or parenting, lying alone in her queen-size bed, wide awake on a dark night and holding this psalm close to her: "The property lines have fallen beautifully for me" (v. 6); "I will bless the LORD who advises me; / even at night I am instructed in the depths of my mind" (v. 7).

Imagining the psalm attached to the story of this specific person causes certain images and certain phrases from the poem to jump out at you; particular verses rise to the top and that makes choosing a controlling image that much easier. In effect, your imagined listener becomes the frame that surrounds your controlling image and allows it to stand out.

Sermons and Image on Screens

I n 1987 two Silicon Valley software engineers named Dennis Austin and Thomas Rudkin were hard at work on a brand-new computer program. They had the idea that they could use the graphical interface of the new Apple Macintosh as a platform for people who wanted to create presentations that combined text and graphics. They called their program Presenter, and together with Robert Gaskins they started a company called Forethought with the intent of bringing their product to the world. Microsoft heard about what they were doing and in 1987 purchased Forethought and added Presenter to its product line under a new name: PowerPoint. In 1990 PowerPoint was fully adapted to the Microsoft operating system and released to the general public.[1]

The communications world has never been the same. Even though the program has been widely available for less than thirty years, it has changed the way information is communicated in all sorts of places, including the church.

Before PowerPoint, some churches already used screens, usually employing an overhead projector. Words of songs or points from the preacher's sermon were projected for the congregation's benefit. Moreover, many congregations used artwork on the covers of worship bulletins, and often this was designed to fit a theme of the day. But the technology used to employ this imagery was rather crude and labor intensive, so its use was limited.

PowerPoint changed all that. Now images, text, color, and even video could be seamlessly integrated into every aspect of the service. Whole new possibilities opened up for preachers and worship leaders, with the result that if you walk into a North American Protestant[2] church today, chances are you will find a screen, a projector, and a computer running some sort of presentational software. Today large churches spend tens of thousands of dollars on technologies associated with screens, and they hire worship arts coordinators and ministers of multimedia to manage that technology. It's arguably the most significant change in worship in the last thirty years, and it's not going away.

Presentational technology has impacted preaching too. Many ministers are integrating screens into their sermons. When they write their sermons, these preachers don't just create a manuscript (or outline) on Microsoft Word, they craft a presentation on PowerPoint.

Benefits of Presentational Technology

Many preachers and liturgists are excited about this new tool. As Marc Newman says, "Humans are visual creatures. Even when stories are communicated orally, they 'appear' in the mind's eye."[3] PowerPoint gives worship leaders a tool that can speak powerfully and directly to that "mind's eye."

Furthermore, we live in a visual age: between televisions, computers, movies, and smartphones, we are immersed in technologies designed to communicate through images. Our children grow up surrounded by screens. Images have become a kind of native language for a whole generation. Paul Scott Wilson has said that one of the imperatives for preachers in this changed world is that they "immerse themselves in the mind-set of today in order to be able to speak creatively to a changed world."[4] Images are clearly part of that contemporary mind-set and presentational technology gives us the means to speak to it.

Another positive side of screen imagery is its ability to speak theopoetically. In his book *Preaching as Poetry*, Paul Scott Wilson calls modern preachers to move away from the communication style of modernity, where rational argument and dogma were the communication staples, and toward what he calls "theopoetic preaching, . . . [which] speaks of God in poetic ways. This is not preaching poems; it is poetic preaching that treasures language—with all of its frail images, symbols, and metaphors—to communicate God."[5] Wilson sees visual language at the center of the theopoetic enterprise, and clearly screens give us a means to communicate on that visual wavelength.

Concerns about Presentational Technology

While some leaders hail presentational technology as the dawn of a new, more powerful age of communication,[6] others are less sure. I teach a class at Calvin Theological Seminary, where John Rottman and Scott Hoezee are the professors of preaching. Like other teachers of preaching who love words and are sensitive to preaching as an oral/aural art, they do not want to detract from God's word being heard as witness and testimony that invites listeners to participate in certain important ways. They are not against screen images, but they point out that when a sermon image is projected on a screen for the listeners, the shape of the image is determined for them. Their imaginations are relatively passive. They don't have to picture what the minister says because it's right there in front of them. All the work is done.

By contrast, a spoken image compels the listeners to paint the picture in their own minds. Because they have work to do, they are more actively engaged in the sermon. My colleagues suggest that participation of the listener in the image creation process leaves a deeper impression than passive reception of an image spoon-fed to them on the screen.

Other criticisms of PowerPoint go back to old concerns about the point-form preaching that used to dominate in what is now sometimes called the Old Homiletic. The movement in preaching has been away from deductive, point-form sermons and toward inductive sermons that emphasize narrative and story.[7] PowerPoint and programs like it are often used to present information in bullet points. Many observers feel that when sermons are offered this way, some of the driest excesses of propositional preaching are returning to the pulpit.

Others have expressed legitimate concerns about the very practical issue of cost. Although prices are falling, the equipment needed to run presentational technology is not cheap, and once the technology is in place, many churches find that people need to run the system on Sunday morning as well as during the week. All churches struggle to fit these new costs into already tight budgets, and small churches are particularly burdened.

Then there are the time concerns. Pastors are busy people. Between writing our sermons, attending our meetings, visiting the sick, conducting funerals and weddings, and managing the church's many programs, we are already spread thin. Preparing a good presentation takes time. Can preachers really afford this time? Is it a good return on their investment?

In the world of secular presentations there has been some backlash too. By 2005 PowerPoint presentations had become so ubiquitous in the business world that people began talking about "death by PowerPoint"; listeners felt as though they were being mercilessly strafed by bullet points fired at them in slide after mind-numbing slide. In 2010 the *New York Times* published an article about the use of presentational technology in the military entitled "We Have Met the Enemy and He Is PowerPoint." It was massively shared by millions of readers who had been through a few too many exhausting presentations. A military commander admitted that PowerPoint was sometimes used during presentations to the press as a way to dull the reporters' minds. They called it "hypnotizing chickens."[8]

Presentational Technology Is Here to Stay

The concerns expressed about PowerPoint are real but probably not fatal. Ministers should be wise in their use of technologies like PowerPoint, but the evil is not in the tool; most likely the evil is in the presenter. For example, there have always been bad sermons. But bad sermons do not prove that the sermon form is terrible and must be discarded; so, too, bad PowerPoint presentations do not prove that presentational technology can't be used to enhance a sermon.

In the end, whether you are all-in on screens or reticent, presentational technology is here to stay. Thousands of churches will use it to present the liturgical elements of a service, and thousands of pastors will use slides as part of the sermon. Several times during my ministry I've been a guest preacher at churches where a screen was simply not available to me as I preached but use of the screen was expected. If I didn't have some sort of visual to accompany my verbiage, the congregation would have felt as though the sermon was incomplete. That's a measure of how deeply screens have nestled themselves into sermon culture.

In this chapter I will not be able to look at all the issues surrounding presentational technology and worship; instead I will restrict myself to guidelines for using screen images within a sermon. While I will certainly talk about the use of text on the screen (particularly the danger of too much text), my primary concern will be with the visuals and pictures chosen for a sermon. In keeping with the theme of the book, I will focus especially on the possibility of using presentational technology as a way to solidify the sermon's controlling image in the imagination of a worshipper.

Keep It Simple: One Theme, One Metaphor

At both churches I've served, worship was planned with a team. Liturgist, music director, and preaching pastor would sit down together and work out the service. These meetings would always begin with the question, "So what's the sermon about?" In good Protestant fashion, the preached word was the center of the service and we wanted everything in the service to be governed by the text for the day. Notice the question was not, "What Bible passage are you preaching on?" It was, "What's the sermon about?" As worship planners we wanted to know what the preacher would do with the text. We wanted to know the sermon theme. More specifically, we wanted to know if there was some sort of governing metaphor that would convey the sermon's theme because we wanted that metaphor to inform the whole liturgy. We wanted that metaphor to shape the hymns, the liturgical readings, and the landscape of the whole service.

So, for example, if I was preaching on Hebrews 12:1-3 ("Let us run with perseverance the race marked out for us," NIV) and the controlling image was about persevering on a long road of pilgrimage, we would look for hymns, readings, and liturgical elements that used traveling imagery. No matter how wonderful a hymn might be, if it didn't have the governing metaphor, it didn't make the service.

When it comes to music, I think many pastors plan worship this way. As we consider the integration of screens and projected imagery into our services, the same level of attention to metaphorical integrity should be applied to the pictures on our screens.

As you read through the criticisms of PowerPoint presentations, you find that critics often complain that the presentations are too busy and lack thematic unity. The images come at you one after another and there seems to be no relation between one image and the next. So, for example, a service begins with announcements and when the kids' programs are announced, pictures of children appear on the screen. Next comes the call to worship accompanied by a picture of a person with her arms upraised toward a purple sunset. During the service of confession the screen fills with a picture of a flowing river sparkling in the sunlight overlaid with the text for the communal prayer. The words of the hymn of response are framed by scenes of mountains bathed in sunlight, while the scripture reading for the day is paired with a dark sky split by the arc of a brilliant rainbow. The sermon features bulleted phases outlining the pastor's points and subpoints on a background of Facebook blue with an understated curlicue in the corner. The slides are text heavy, with the occasional map or picture of Ephesus or image of Jesus thrown in.

I would suggest that such a service is, visually speaking, a thematic mess. It is the visual equivalent of a service where the hymns are a patchwork of styles and themes; a service where "Praise, My Soul, the King of Heaven" is followed immediately by "Jesus Wants Me for a Sunbeam." We would never chose our music that way; we shouldn't handle our images that way either.

Although it's a secular book and aimed chiefly at executives and salespeople who make presentations in the corporate realm, Garr Reynolds's *Presentation Zen* is an interesting read for all preachers, especially ones who want to integrate presentational imagery into their message. Reynolds laments hours wasted in soul-killing business presentations where bad PowerPoints made the talks worse instead of better. His mantra throughout the book is simplicity. In one section, using a metaphor from the world of radio broadcasting, he urges presenters to strive for the highest signal-to-noise ratio (SNR) possible. In radio a high signal-to-noise ratio means the voice of the broadcaster is clear and strong, while the background hiss is virtually nonexistent. In the visual realm,

> The goal is to have the highest signal-to-noise ratio possible in your slides. People have a hard time coping with too much information. There is simply a limit to a person's ability to process new information efficiently and effectively. Aiming at a higher SNR attempts to make things easier for people. Understanding can be hard enough without bombarding audience members with excessive and nonessential bombardment by our visuals that are supposed to be playing a supporting role.[9]

The Controlling Image and Potential Screen Images

When a preacher and the worship team sit down to plan the service, the sermon theme and the controlling image for that sermon should be available to all the planners. As far as possible, all the slides should be chosen with that image front and center. While there can be images that play with different aspects of the main metaphor, there shouldn't be any images that point away from that metaphor.

For example, if you are preaching on Hebrews 12 and using the race/pilgrimage image, during a call to confession you might have some imagery of people struggling along or hesitating on the path, or you could have images of broad highways juxtaposed with narrow and difficult paths. Later in the service, when you are moving toward an assurance of God bringing us across the finish line, you could have images of people coming home, or finishing a race, or standing on top of a mountain after the hike. There is still room for creativity and variety, but the controlling image should set metaphorical boundaries.

In their book *The Wired Church 2.0*, Len Wilson and Jason Moore make the same point. They suggest that worship planners

> look for a central image that communicates the idea or theme for the entire worship service. . . . Once a singular focus for the day has been decided, all aspects of worship can be built on variations of that common visual theme. . . .
>
> If you want people who come to worship to "get it" and take "it" home with them, creating a single image that represents the metaphor, and thus the theme, for the day can be very helpful. Ideally this main image would be displayed even before the worship starts. It would appear in between songs, before and after video and music clips, and any other time there isn't another image that makes sense. . . . Consider it a default image.[10]

Not only should the images have a certain visual unity, but also most presentation experts warn against too many slides. Guy Kawasaki is a venture capitalist and an entrepreneur who has been working in Silicon Valley since the mid-eighties. He speaks regularly, he's written books on the art of persuasion, and, by his own account, he has attended thousands of presentations in his lifetime. So many of those presentations were overstuffed that in a 2005 blog post he proposed what he called the 10/20/30 rule. Kawasaki says that a presenter should use only ten slides, he should talk for only twenty minutes, and he should never use less than a thirty-point font.[11] Kawasaki's rule is obviously aimed at achieving visual simplicity. Most presentations have too many bullet points, contain too many images, and leave the viewer/listener feeling buried.

It's a little like many of the sermons written by beginning preachers. The eager young preacher spends hours studying the text and gathering insights. Every single one of those insights seems good to the exegete, and so the sermon shares all of them. When the message is delivered, the congregation feels like they've just been on a twenty-minute Tilt-A-Whirl ride. They feel as though they've just been buried in information. This is why homiletics professors and homiletics textbooks are constantly telling preachers, "Make your sermon about one thing, one big idea, one theme!" When it comes to written sermons, beginning preachers need to learn the lesson of simplicity. They need to apply the same lesson to the visual side. Keep your presentations simple.

In contrast to the visual mess that I've experienced in sermons where screens are used, I recently saw a positive use of PowerPoint in a sermon, a use that observed the rule of simplicity. Heidi DeJonge is a pastor in Kingston, Ontario, Canada. She preached on Genesis 24 and the story of Abraham's servant's journey to find a wife for Isaac. She called her sermon "Love at First Sight," and it centered on the idea that Rebekah's willingness to offer a drink both to Abraham's servant and to his camels was an echo of the kind of self-giving love that God constantly pours out on his people. Reverend DeJonge said that Rebekah showed the best kind of love at first sight: as soon as she saw the servant's need she ministered to that need and did it quickly. This is a very different kind of love at first sight from the kind usually celebrated by our culture. In our culture's portrayal of love at first sight, two people who see each other suddenly feel the spark of attraction. Eros flames and they are instantly drawn to one another. This is a love at first sight based on the beauty of the other; Rebekah's love at first sight is more like the unconditional, agapic love of God.

To make this point visually, DeJonge used two video clips. At the beginning of the sermon she showed a clip from the 1996 movie *Romeo and Juliet* starring Claire Danes and Leonardo DiCaprio, a movie that put Shakespeare's play in a contemporary setting. She showed a one-minute scene where Romeo and Juliet see each other for the first time. They catch a glimpse of one another through an aquarium and for almost a full minute they gaze in wonder at the other, exchanging flirtatious smiles and generally smoldering. It's love at first sight.

DeJonge didn't condemn this romantic attraction, she simply noted how the love at the center of Genesis 24, the love Rebekah showed when she watered the servant's camels, was a little different. She illustrated that love with a film clip from the country of Norway. A young boy was on a bench waiting for a bus in the middle of winter. He was very clearly underdressed, wearing only a light sweatshirt, jeans, and tennis shoes. He shivered miserably and the camera recorded the reaction of people as they came upon this situation of need. How many people would help the boy? Many bystanders simply ignored the child and went about their own business, but a few gave him gloves, offered a scarf, or in some cases took off their own coats and threw them around the boy. DeJonge said that these people, like Rebekah, showed love at first sight. The sermon concluded with her anchoring this love in God's love at first sight for us, that unconditional love of God that is wrapped around our shivering shoulders every single day.

There is admirable simplicity here: two clear video clips, carefully chosen to illustrate the theme and the controlling image of the sermon. There were no other video clips in the sermon and very few other images. In between the images, when there was no need for an image on the screen, the words "Love at First Sight" were displayed, thus reinforcing the sermon theme and image. Even screen skeptics and PowerPoint curmudgeons would have to admit that DeJonge used these images in a way that enhanced the gospel message.

A Good Screen Image Needs You

Have you been to this presentation? A man comes to preach or make a presentation in your church's adult education hour. He's worked really hard on a slide show to accompany his words. There are fifty slides, packed with charts, graphs, bullet points, and, of course, pictures. In a well-intentioned effort to make the slides as informative has possible, every slide is packed with information. In fact, you could probably get the whole gist of the presentation simply by watching the slides.

This is very bad. When all the material is on the slide, the presider inevitably spends half of the sermon/presentation reading the slides. A new slide pops up and he or she turns away from you, the audience, toward the screen to read the self-explanatory bullet point. Then, after reading it, the presenter turns toward you and explains the point again, this time in his or her own words, even though you got the point when you read the information on the screen. In effect you are whacked by the same information three times in a row! You first get the message as soon as the slide comes up, because before the speaker says a word you read it and get the point. But then, even though you've already read it yourself, the presenter reads the slide again, so you've been hit a second time. By the time the point is explained for a third time, this time in the presenter's own words, your eyes are starting to glaze and you find yourself wondering if the Detroit Tigers will beat the Kansas City Royals in major-league baseball this afternoon.

Most presentation experts agree: your slides should have enough information to intrigue and *begin* to inform your audience, but there should be some mystery left over, some questions unanswered. Garr Reynolds quotes David Rose, another expert presenter, who offers this advice:

> Never, ever hand out copies of your slides, and certainly not before your presentation. That is the kiss of death. By definition, since slides are "speaker support" material, they are in support of the speaker . . . YOU. As such, they should be completely incapable of standing by themselves, and are thus useless to give to your audience, where they will simply be guaranteed to be a distraction. The flip side of this is that if the slides can stand by themselves, why the heck are you up in front of them?[12]

Later in the book Reynolds offers visual examples of what he means.[13] A presenter is trying to illustrate the point that in Japan, women make up the vast majority of the part-time labor force: 72 percent of the part-time workers in Japan are women. The first slide Reynolds shows to illustrate this point looks something like this (I created my own slide, but it is laid out much like Reynolds's example):

According to the Ministry of Labor, 72% of the part-time workers in Japan are women.

Gender Issues in Japan

Image courtesy of ankomando/Shutterstock.com

Reynolds sees this as an ineffective image. He points out how the clip art is rather dull and the slide is text heavy. More important, the slide is problematic because it tells you everything you need to know. There is no mystery left. The speaker has nothing to do.

In contrast, Reynolds offers this slide as a better example. Again, his is slightly different, but my modifications are essentially the same.

72%

Image courtesy of takayuki/Shutterstock.com

This is a much better slide because it is simple, text light, and more vital. It needs you, the speaker, to explain it. You look at it and there is enough information to solidify your point in the audience's mind after you've spoken, but the image by itself makes the viewer wonder, *What's that 72 percent all about?* Instead of shutting down inquiry, the slide causes the viewer to lean forward, eager to hear the new information that only you can supply.[14]

Kenton Anderson, professor of homiletics at Northwest Baptist Theological Seminary, sums it up this way:

> The most effective slides are pleasing to the eye, matching a relevant image or graphic with a minimum of words. The point of the screen is to complement the speaker, not to compete with what the preacher is saying.[15]

Use Propulsive Images, Not Clichés

Here are a couple of guidelines for pastors and worship leaders as they search for screen images to accompany worship:

> Use compelling material. Make sure that every image, video or word you use is going to enhance the presentation and its impact on the worship experience. The audience is not interested in looking at images just tossed onto a screen.[16]

Quality counts when using slides. People are accustomed to seeing high quality graphics and images. . . . You do not want to inadvertently signal that your church is backward or inattentive by showing slip-shod visuals on the screen. If that is the best that you are capable of, it might be worth asking whether you ought to be showing anything at all.[17]

Both of these writers are on to something. They recognize that some images on the screen work while others fall flat. They fail to grab our attention, they fail to touch our imaginations, and sometimes they even deaden our imaginative faculties. As Steve Koster writes, "Poor choices for backgrounds can quickly become distracting to worship rather than beneficial. A cliche sunset or awkward photograph becomes a stumbling block, particularly if it occurs often."[18] In other words, a PowerPoint with bad images is worse than no PowerPoint at all.

But how can you distinguish a good image, one that is compelling and propelling and has an impact on the worship experience, from an image that is an imagination-killing cliché? We all know that some images propel the imagination while others simply sit on the surface of our senses; how can we have more propulsion and less sitting?

Icons as Images That Propel

Instead of turning to modern advice, let's look to an ancient source to help us answer this question. In some ways, even though they would never use digital media in their worship, the Orthodox Church with its tradition of icons can be a great help in thinking about this question. After all, they have spent almost two thousand years reflecting on imagery as an aid to worship. Orthodox worship has always been multisensory and perhaps none of those senses has been as well attended as sight.

Of course, icons in the Orthodox Church are highly stylized. There is nearly always a dome over the church featuring the image of Christ looking down with his hand upraised in blessing. There is an iconostasis in front of the church. An iconostasis is an architectural screen that separates the church nave from the sanctuary. It has three doors. The holy door is central and the doors to the left and the right are called the deacons' doors. The entire iconostasis is covered with icons and placement of those icons follows prescribed patterns. The holy doors are flanked on the right by an icon of Christ holding an open Bible and on the left by an image of Mary holding an infant Jesus. There is often an image of John the Baptist to Jesus's right, and somewhere on the iconostasis the patron saint for whom the church is named is also pictured. At the center of the iconostasis are the holy doors that lead to the altar. An image of the angel Gabriel coming to Mary in the annunciation is typically placed on those doors. If you walk through the holy doors (and only a few people are allowed to do that), you will see the altar. High above the altar will likely be an image of Mary with Christ on her lap, her arms outstretched in prayerful blessing on the church. Here's an image from Tornio Orthodox Church, Tornio, Finland, to illustrate.

Iconostasis of Tornio Orthodox Church, Tornio, Finland. Photo: Mikael Lindmark

There are variations on these themes. The icons of Christ and Mary beside the holy doors don't look the same in every church, and this variety creates differences in emphasis and tone, but there are consistent visual elements that anchor the worship space. These icons are absolutely central to the worship of Orthodox believers. They are meant to propel the imagination and touch the spirit. The icons are not worshipped, but they lead the Orthodox believer to worship the spiritual reality they depict.

When Protestants like me first comes into contact with icons, we are struck by how strange they are. The people depicted in the icons are not portrayed realistically. Their faces are elongated. Their noses are especially stretched and thin. The icons seem to pay little or no attention to the rules of perspective: the edges of the table at the Lord's Supper don't move toward a vanishing point; all the images seem flat compared to perspective-driven western painting. A Protestant viewer used to the conventions of western painting might well think, *What's the matter with these icon painters? Don't they know how to draw a realistic human face? Don't they know how to use perspective?*

Of course they know. The strangeness of the icons is intentional. The iconographer shapes the image so that its peculiarities are precisely what give the image its spiritual power. Frederica Mathewes-Green, a midlife convert to Orthodoxy, talks about this in her book *The Open Door*:

> For a long time I didn't like icons at all. They didn't appeal to me; they didn't even make sense. When other people talked about how beautiful and moving icons were, I'd arrange my features into a thoughtful, serious expression, but inside I'd be thinking, "I have no idea what they're talking about."
>
> Icons seemed to me the opposite of appealing. The art looked like bad art, with clumsy perspective and unrealistic faces. Worst of all, icons didn't convey emotion. Everyone looked so stiff and unfriendly. When it came to religious art, I much preferred to stroll of the halls of the National Gallery of Art and view color-saturated canvases from the Renaissance, full of plump babies and yearning eyes cast upwards. Art that showed people who looked like real people, portrayed in ways that tugged the heartstrings.[19]

Christ Pantocrator, Saint Catherine's Monastery, Mount Sinai

But over time Mathewes-Green's opinions changed. Now she realizes that when the icons unsettled her Protestant mind, that discomfort was already a sign of the images' power. Now she opens herself up to what is challenging and strange in icons as a spiritual exercise. For example, she spends time with a famous icon, the *Christ of Sinai*, and shows how that image works on the viewer. Here's the image: Mathewes-Green makes several keen observations about this icon.

First of all, as with many icons, the image is unsettling because Jesus is looking straight at you, and he's looking with a penetrating rather than vacant gaze. The effect is doubly strong because his eyes are unusually large, much larger proportionately than "realistic" human eyes, and that intensifies his gaze. You can't seem to escape those eyes.

Furthermore each eye is a little different. Try this exercise. Cover the left half of Jesus's face (the darker half) with your finger and look only at the right half of his face. What expression do you see there? Most people would say, "Something like tenderness or compassion." You see here a Jesus who knows your pain. Now cover the right half of Jesus's face and look only at the left half. It's different, isn't it? Most people call the expression on the left side of his face "stern" or "confrontational." You see here a Jesus who knows that you are not yet the person you could be, and he's calling you to justice and righteousness. The effect is striking, and when you look closely, you can see it's intentional. The artist has slightly varied the shape of the eye, the shape of the eyebrow, and even the shape of Jesus's lips in order to create the effect.

The overall effect is so strong that Mathewes-Green writes how an unbelieving humanities professor who knew her husband was given a copy of this icon. After living with it for a while he went to her husband in frustration. "When I look at it, I have the sensation that He's looking into my soul. Before this, I didn't even think there was such a thing as a soul."[20]

When an Orthodox Church leader wants to put an image of Jesus up in church, he does the opposite of finding a stock image of Jesus to slap up in the sanctuary. An icon never says simply, "Here's Jesus," "Here's Mary," or "Here's John the Baptist." Instead the images are chosen and crafted in such a way that they push you, transport you. "In a way that's hard to define, icons touch a completely different interior level," says Mathewes-Green, "something below the hectic region of thought and emotion. Deeper down there is a place where we first confront life, before we decide what we think and feel about it."[21]

The construction and impact of icons in the early church can teach us something about the choice and use of screen images in the digital-age church. The images we put on the screen should not be dull, flat, didactic pictures that show what's obvious and expected. Either by the way they are composed or the manner in which they are framed, they should push us, unsettle us, astonish us, move us, surprise us. In the words of Mathewes-Green, they should aim to touch that deeper-down region, the region below thought and emotion, where we first confront life.

Connotative and Denotative Images

This is what all art aims for. Artists want to produce work that is connotative.

Some pictures are merely denotative: Here is a picture of a dog. Here is a picture of Jerusalem. Here is a picture of my house. Sometimes images aim to reflect physical reality as clearly and accurately as possible, like a fifth-grader who sits down to draw the piece of fruit that his teacher has placed on the table in front of class; he tries to make a drawing that looks just like the apple. There is nothing wrong with these simple, straightforward pictures. They have a purpose. They educate. They inform. But artists shoot for more than that. Artists don't just want to denote, they want to connote.

The artist will do something with a still life to make it more than a straight copy. Vincent van Gogh painted his bedroom apartment in Arles, France, but he didn't paint it plain; instead he played with the colors and the perspective so that they arrest the viewer and touch something deeper within the viewer, causing him or her to stop and wonder what's going on.

Vincent van Gogh, *Van Gogh's Bedroom in Arles*, Musée d'Orsay, Paris, France

110

Too many of the screen images chosen to illustrate sermons are merely denotative. The preacher talks about the tabernacle, so he or she throws an image of the tabernacle up on the screen. Then the preacher talks about the giving the law and shows a stock picture of Charlton Heston holding the Ten Commandments. Then the preacher talks about the Pharisees, and he or she finds a picture of Pharisee-like people on Google Images (sandals and robes and flowing beards, I suppose) and puts that up on the screen. Finally the preacher talks about Jesus fulfilling the Law and the screen glows with a stock photo of Christ smiling beneficently over the congregation. Are any of these images wrong or misleading? No. But they're terribly unimaginative. They are the visual equivalent of one of those canned sermons stories you can get out of a *1001 Moving Sermon Illustrations* book, stories that begin, "Once upon a time there was a little boy who didn't want to go to church."

Listeners' minds grow slack when preachers use these canned illustrations because they are predictable and the listener feels as though he or she already knows exactly how the story will end. In the same way, people's eyes glaze over when didactic, predictable images are all they see on the screen. As preachers we need to develop an artist's eye for angularity and depth so that we can choose images for screens that arrest the attention, that unsettle our listeners, that cause them to lean forward in their seats, eager to hear what we have to say.

In a convergence full of common grace, the wisdom found in the ancient artistry of the iconographers is echoed by the people who are thinking most carefully about presentational technology in the business world. "Cheesy metaphors are a cop-out," states Nancy Duarte, and if in choosing an image to represent cooperation "you feel tempted to use a picture of two hands shaking in front of a globe, put the pencil down, step away from the desk, and think about taking a vacation or investigating aromatherapy."[22]

Speaker and author Seth Godin gets very specific when he describes how he wants a slide to work in his presentations: "You put up a slide. It triggers an emotional reaction in the audience. They sit up and want to know what you're going to say that fits in with that image. Then, if you do it right, every time they think of what you said, they'll see the image (and vice versa)."[23] Clearly, Godin is aiming at both mystery and connotative depth when he chooses an image and constructs a slide. He wants the slide to both inform and raise questions. He wants an image that touches the imagination and wakes up the intellect.

Finding a Propulsive Picture

Let's look at some examples of how this looks in practice. Let's suppose you are preaching a sermon on Psalm 8 and the theme you've chosen is "God sees and cares for us even though we are small creatures." Your theme comes from verses 3-4, which say,

> When I look up at your skies,
>   at what your fingers made—
> the moon and the stars
>   that you set firmly in place—
> what are human beings
>   that you think about them;
> what are human beings
>   that you pay attention to them?

As a goal of the sermon you want the congregation to get a sense of their frailty, to see and feel it, and you want an image that conveys their smallness. You want an image that both denotes and connotes this theme. What sort of image might you choose?

You could choose an image of a typical human being, perhaps with a question mark over the top of it. The question in the text is "What are human beings?" so why not picture a human, maybe like this:

What are
Human Beings?

Image courtesy of mimagephotography/Shutterstock.com

It's a serviceable image. It's a picture of a generic person and at least she has something like a questioning look on her face. But there's not much here to really grab the imagination, and there's nothing here that would create a sense of wonder and open up questions in the mind of the viewer. Here's an improvement:

Image courtesy of Balazs Kovacs Images/Shutterstock.com

The expression on the man's face is much more searching and vulnerable, the single question mark is more evocative than the text-heavy sentence, and the deep shadows make the image more serious and penetrating. It's better, but still not great.

Perhaps an image of a child would improve things:

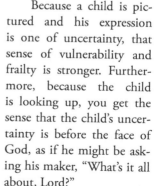

Because a child is pictured and his expression is one of uncertainty, that sense of vulnerability and frailty is stronger. Furthermore, because the child is looking up, you get the sense that the child's uncertainty is before the face of God, as if he might be asking his maker, "What's it all about, Lord?"

Image courtesy of Sukhonosova Anatasia/Shutterstock.com

Perhaps you could take the imagery in an entirely different direction: instead of picturing the frailty of the human, why not show the majesty of the heavens. After all, the psalmist knows his frailty when he sets his life against the expanse of the stars. Perhaps a slide with a human being standing under the dome of the stars looking up in wonder with the words *When I consider the works of your hands* . . . underneath it? That would put the congregation in the place of the psalmist as they listen to the sermon.

But my favorite image for this presentation would definitely be a famous picture taken from the edge of our solar system by the Voyager spacecraft in 1990.[24]

In 1990 Voyager had traveled 6 billion miles, but before it left the solar system's outer limit NASA engineers ordered it to take a picture of Earth. From this distance our planet appears as a tiny speck framed in the rays of sunlight refracted by the camera lens. The speck is so small, it's hard to pick up in the photograph. The picture is known as the *Pale Blue Dot*, and it's an iconic image of our planet's frailty.

Upon seeing the picture, Carl Sagan wrote:

> Consider again that dot. That's here. That's home. That's us. On it everyone you love, everyone you know, everyone you ever heard of, every human being who ever was, lived out their lives. The aggregate of our joy and suffering, thousands of confident religions, ideologies, and economic doctrines, every hunter and forager, every hero and coward, every creator and destroyer of civilization, every king and peasant, every young couple in love, every mother and father, hopeful child, inventor and explorer, every teacher of morals, every corrupt politician, every "superstar," every "supreme leader," every saint and sinner in the history of our species lived there—on a mote of dust suspended in a sunbeam.[25]

"What are human beings that you think about them?" (Ps 8:4). The *Pale Blue Dot* image is propulsive. It's the kind of picture that people won't forget. It's the kind of picture that explodes in the imagination. This picture opens our hearts and minds to our smallness against the reaches of space and our brevity beside the great sweep of time. That God's love in Jesus Christ reaches down through the vast reaches of space, all the way down to that pale blue dot and somehow finds us, is good news of great joy for all people.

Image selection is not an exact science. Life experience and personal taste have a lot to do with how an image impacts a person. But a little reflection shows that there are ways to make the pictures that accompany our sermons memorable. As worship media specialist Eileen Crowley puts it, "When the media in worship stands on its own and is designed in such a way as to invite viewers into active participation in its interpretation, media moves beyond being simply an element of presentation technology and becomes what may legitimately be called media art."[26]

Pay Attention to Images and Context

I grew up in Kingston, Ontario, Canada. It's a lovely town nestled on the eastern end of the great lakes, right where the waters of Lake Ontario empty into the Saint Lawrence River. Kingston is a university town. The largest employer is Queens University, and the Royal Military College of Canada is also in town. It's also a tourist town. The downtown area is filled with early nineteenth-century limestone buildings, many of them inhabited by coffee shops, cozy restaurants, used bookstores, and unique retail outlets.

Perhaps because of its university pedigree, Kingston is not much of a hunting town. There's not much of a gun culture, and in the circles in which I moved, nobody went hunting. Fishing, yes. Hunting, not so much.

I now live in western Michigan, and hunting is huge here. When the season arrives, it seems like half the people I know pick up a gun or a bow and head off into the woods. Most of the time I find large areas of overlap between the cultures of western Michigan and eastern Ontario, but hunting is one of the few areas in which they diverge.

When I was a teenager, our eastern Ontario church welcomed a new minister who came from western Michigan. He was a wonderful man who served the church well for many years. But I remember that in one of his early sermons he wanted to make a point about waiting, and to illustrate that point he used a deer-hunting story.

He talked about going hunting with his uncles when he was a teenager. After putting on his gear and getting his gun, they trudged out into the woods where he was told to sit in a tree stand and wait. And wait he did. For hours he sat in the tree stand surveying the woods and trying to stay warm. The only wildlife to come near his stand were a few squirrels.

But then just as he was getting tired, just when he thought this hunting thing was for the birds, he heard a rustle in the underbrush and walking right toward him through the woods was a big, beautiful, ten-point buck. His heart started to pound. As quietly and slowly as possible he raised his gun to his shoulder. He took aim at the magnificent animal and pulled the trigger. It was a clean hit! His waiting had been rewarded. On his first outing with his uncles, he had brought down a ten-point buck!

115

Our new pastor told the story with cheerful excitement. But to me, a teenager who had been raised in a nonhunting culture where a deer sighting was a very rare thing indeed, this story was an ecological tragedy! My new pastor had killed Bambi! I can still remember that as he told the story, because of my context I expected him to end it by saying something like: "The deer was so beautiful and noble! I just couldn't shoot, so I let him go, free to roam the woods, and I went back to my uncles empty-handed." When he chose instead to pull the trigger, I was horrified. The young minister intended his story to function as an image for patience and reward. In the context of my eastern Ontario church, in the ears of most of the listeners, it had a completely different effect.

Many of the images that we choose to anchor a sermon will have universal appeal. I think the pale blue dot would work in any context. But because every church community's context is unique, every church will also have a certain set of images unique to its setting, and the members will receive even the "universal" images in a slightly different way. To put it more technically: the connotative meaning of the images that you choose for your sermons will vary from church to church. At the time of this writing, Barack Obama is president of the United States. A screen image of President Obama will bring one kind of emotional response in Nairobi, Kenya, and another kind of response in rural Alabama. In my western Michigan context, a Detroit Lions football club logo would be a vivid symbol of pain, frustration, and dashed hopes. In most other parts of the United States and Canada, it would have a completely different connotative meaning.

If you really want to choose effective images for your sermons, you need to pay close attention to your context. If you want to find images that connect, you need to know the lives and stories of the people to whom you are preaching: What books do they read, what movies do they watch, what television shows do they talk about in the church narthex, what are their favorite vacation places, what do they love, what do they fear? You need to balance images of men and women, different ages and races. You need to be sensitive to economic issues and politics and be careful to avoid stereotypes. Of course, all preachers need to do this, not just those using screen images. However, preachers using images are more likely to transgress because good pictures are harder to find. Images are a little like a language and when it comes to the language of images, every local church has its own dialect. We need to learn and speak the dialect.

That's what Jesus did. Jesus didn't use screens, but he did use images, and when he used images he spoke in the vernacular. These images were all familiar to his listeners:

- the farmer sowing his seed

- the shepherd looking for a lost sheep

- the shock of the father running to meet his prodigal son

- the contrast between the tiny mustard seed and its abundant plant

- the two sparrows sold for a penny

- the maidens waiting for the groom at a wedding banquet

- the Pharisee praying proudly in the temple

All of these were images firmly grounded in local experience. Readers from different cultures and times can *begin* to understand them, but the fullness of the connotative impact upon Jesus's original hearers now needs explanation. The preacher has to tell us how scandalous it was for a father to run to a son so that we can understand the connotations of the parable. For a local, those connotations would have immediate impact. Jesus used pictures that came from his local context and as a result his sermons had a deep impact.

Local Imagery

Some leaders in worship arts take sensitivity to context a step further. They recommend that churches create their own local images. Instead of always running to Google Images for your sermon visuals, why not find a team of artists and photographers from your congregation, young and old, men and women, all of them fluent in your local image dialect, who are willing to go out and take pictures that capture the theme of the sermon?

Eileen Crowley has written extensively on this. She advocates a model of media ministry called Communal Co-Creation. It involves forming teams of people who are gifted in areas like design and the visual arts to help pastors make good choices for their visual presentations. These teams can also create images specific to an individual sermon, service, or season.[27] In my own denomination, the Christian Reformed Church, Marc Nelesen and Darrin Sculley led the members of their church in some intentional reflection on using screens in worship. When it came to the use of artwork the committee decided that images should be soft and sensitive to the "space" as holy ground. Art should be coordinated with the worship décor committee and sensitive to the other areas in the worship space and liturgical season. *Where possible, we would like to see the AV committee use commissioned rather than "stock" iconographic images.*[28]

In his book *Actuality: Stories of Real Life for Sermons That Matter*, Scott Hoezee tells of hearing a presentation in which sociologist Roman Williams gathered data for his studies by giving people cameras and asking them to record events and images from their regular lives. Instead of collecting data in a text-based survey, Williams's survey would be composed of images. Hoezee imagined this same technique applied to sermon preparation.

> Imagine a pastor providing cameras to various members of his or her congregation as a way to gain a virtual window into the lives of the very people to whom he or she preaches every Sunday morning. It is not difficult to see how quickly a pastor would gain a fuller sense of what people do every day and what situations of trouble they regularly face in ways that would almost certainly have an impact on the specificity of examples and stories the preacher could bring into sermons when trying to describe real-life situations of need, want, or hardship as we are thinking of these things in this chapter.[29]

Hoezee imagines these images being translated into verbal examples, but a preacher who uses screens could easily use the images themselves as a way to capture both the trouble and the grace that flows in the lives of their local church members.

Producing your own images is obviously labor intensive. Not all churches will have the volunteer resources to produce liturgical art week after week. Nevertheless, for special services and maybe for select liturgical seasons, locally produced art can be a powerful way to make sure that the images on your screens speak the image dialect of the people in your pews.

This approach needs balance. As fruitful as locally produced imagery might be, if all your pictures come from the lives of your congregation you run the risk of provincialism. Just as a preacher must make sure that the written words of a sermon lift the eyes of the congregation beyond local concerns to issues of global justice and need, so, too, the images chosen to accompany sermons must reflect the global sweep of trouble and the global reach of God's grace.

Develop Files of Images

Almost all preachers develop the skill of collecting stories and illustrations. When it comes to story we become predatory. We read a great passage in a book and say, "Wow! That could work in a sermon!" We see a gripping scene in a movie—let's say the concluding communion scene in *Places in the Heart*—and we think, *Man! That will preach!* During a social outing with friends someone tells an interesting story and we say, "That would fit in a sermon on compassion. Can I use that?" We are constantly on the prowl.

Not only do we prowl, once we find these illustrations we develop effective ways of filing these illustrations for future use. Some of us use traditional paper files and manila folders, some of us scratch a few words down on three-by-five cards, and the most computer-savvy pastors use electronic tools to collect their ideas. These files become invaluable when the time comes to write a sermon.

If we serve a church where screen images are a regular part of the sermon, worship leaders need to develop a similar instinct for images. We need to become image prowlers. We need to get to the point where we see an image in the newspaper, or we see a striking picture in a blog, or we see a poignant scene in a movie, and we start to imagine how that image would look on a screen during our sermon. Once we recognize them, we need to find effective ways of retaining and organizing these images so that when we're writing that sermon on compassion, we will be able to open our "compassion" folder and find a whole group of images, images that that have the connotative power to evoke compassion.

In addition to files based on subjects, a preacher could choose to file according to images of trouble and images of grace. In my own recording system, I have a verbal file for trouble stories and a verbal file for grace stories. For years, whenever I read any account of God doing something good and beautiful in the world, I would reference it and place it in my file of grace stories. In the same way, when I read a story that captures some aspect of the world's brokenness in a particularly angular and poignant way, I put that in my trouble file. The same practice can easily be adapted for images. Everyday images of loss and of hope are paraded before our eyes. Pastors can develop instincts to collect and file those images.

Or images could be collected according to texts. Elizabeth Steele Halstead is the resource specialist for visual arts at the Calvin Institute for Christian Worship. She is a liturgical artist. When she reads a biblical text, she starts to see pictures. Over time she has developed files of digital images related to all sorts of topical and biblical subjects. She has an artist's eye

119

and favors images that are open-ended, connotative, and evocative rather than didactic and obvious. A good example of her work and a model for how images can be collected, tagged with keywords, and filed with texts is found in the Worship Institute's commentary on Philippians, called *Dwelling with Philippians*.[30] This commentary includes not only the more traditional exegetical insights you find in regular commentaries but also poetry and artwork that help listeners envision those exegetical insights. Halstead curated the images in that commentary so that pastors would have a ready-made image file for a sermon on any text of Paul's letter. It's a good example of how our thinking about sermon preparation might change when screens are involved.

Differences between Static Images and Video Clips

As preachers and worship leaders choose images, they should be aware of some of the differences between static images and video clips. Both kinds are evocative, but they work on the viewer in slightly different ways.

Video is what Marshall McLuhan calls a "hot medium." Film clips work directly on the imagination of the viewer and because of their immediacy they exert a strong pull. Due to their "heat," preachers should generally avoid long video clips in the middle of their sermons. Marc Newman suggests that mid-sermon clips be limited to a couple of minutes. Anything longer than that would work best either in the sermon's introduction as an attention getter, or at the end where the "heat" of the story could function as an effective concluding device.[31] If clips are too long and involved, they can carry the viewer away from the plot of the sermon and into the plot of the movie or television program depicted in the clip. If your congregation spends your whole sermon wondering about how the movie ended, it's safe to say your film clip was too "hot."

Static screen images are not as "hot" as images in film, but while they lack film's immediate intensity, they can have an evocative power that is in some ways stronger. Virginia Postrel has noted how still images plucked out of the narrative flow of an old movie can stir up the imagination in ways in which a complete viewing can't. Marilyn Monroe holding down her skirt while standing over a steam grate in *Some Like It Hot*; Audrey Hepburn as Holly Golightly in *Breakfast at Tiffany's*, staring at the camera with her cigarette holder in hand and pearls around her neck; or for my generation, the static image of Luke Skywalker standing poised with his light saber in hand—these are iconic shots that create associations and feelings that a viewing of the whole movie just can't. Postrel says, "Such images lift scenes out of the narrative flow, intensifying their grace and, with it, their glamour."[32] It's the same dynamic that makes some married people more inclined toward still shots of their wedding than videos. The still shots give more freedom for the imagination to roam, for the viewer to explore his or her associations with the images. Film clips are a "hotter" medium, but they give less freedom to the imagination. They intensify feeling but shut down some imaginative associations that a viewer might have.

Preachers and worship leaders working with screens must understand the different nuances of feeling and emotion that these two media have and then learn to use them accordingly.

The Word Comes First

"Liturgical art is different," says Eileen Crowley. "It's not merely the incorporation of media technology, sights and sounds in worship. This liturgical art is media *of* worship. It is not just media *in* worship, but rather it is media integral to the liturgical actions and interactions of the faith community."[33]

Because it is such a powerful medium, presentational technology can take over. Instead of being an aid to worship, the technology enthrones itself as the center of the service and all the other parts of the worship—the sermon, the singing, the prayers—have to adjust themselves to fit the demands of the screen and the technology that illumines it. Crowley says that when this happens, we are getting things backwards.

The liturgy of the church is the starting point. Screen images work best when they are a servant of the liturgical traditions of the local church rather than a master. Of course the use of a screen will affect traditions, and any preachers who institute visuals in their sermons will soon find themselves with slightly altered liturgy, but when the screen is a servant, the changes will be slow and incremental and appropriate.

As I said in chapter 1, sermons should have an image statement as well as a theme. The exegesis of the word comes first. The theme arises out of the exegesis. The controlling image comes next and it reflects the theme. The image is a servant of the text and the theme.

The word comes first. That's worth remembering again as I draw this book to a close. For six chapters we have been talking about the craft of writing a sermon. For six chapters you have heard about things that you can do as a preacher to make your sermons more impactful. We've talked about how a good image propels a sermon. We've talked about how a well-chosen visual can cut the listener to the heart. We've studied the crafts of poets and advertisers to see if we can learn from them. All of this can leave the impression that we preachers are the ones doing the heavy lifting here; as if our words, our images are changing people, as if our imaginative brilliance is keeping the church afloat.

This is very bad. "We have this treasure in clay pots so that the awesome power belongs to God and doesn't come from us" (2 Cor 4:7). When we think of ourselves as the power source, not only do we get the theology wrong, it's a sure recipe for self-destruction. A pastor who thinks he or she has to generate the fire Sunday after Sunday will soon be depressed and burned-out. Our sermon writing and all the craft we bring to it are a humble offering laid at God's feet, and every week, at every stage of the sermon-writing process we pray, "Lord, have mercy." Every week we pray that God will give us some piece of insight to inspire us at the beginning, that God will give us stamina to turn that insight into a sermon, and that God will be with us as we anxiously try to present our insight to the congregation. No matter what their level of craft, most pastors I know are never more conscious of their need of God as when they are producing a sermon.

So we know the word comes first, but we also know our craft is part of it. We know that, in God's providence, God has put treasure in our clay jars, calling ordinary men and women to get up on Sunday mornings and speak the word as best they can. So all week long we work out our sermons with fear and trembling, knowing that it is God who works in us to will and to do, glad to be a small part of the Spirit's glorious work.

Conclusion

In his preface to The Artistry of Preaching book series of which this volume is a part, Paul Scott Wilson writes, "Preaching is much more than art, yet by ensuring that we as preachers employ artistry in our preaching, we assist the Holy Spirit in communicating the gospel to a new generation of people seeking God." I couldn't agree more.

We began this book standing over the beautiful mess of our exegesis. We began pondering the huge pile of insights and associations that the Spirit stirs in us after we study scripture with the intensity and depth that our exegetical tools allow. There is no greater responsibility and no greater joy than the task of taking that beautiful mess and making it into a sermon for hungry people. That craft will take all of our skill and art, and it will require mastery of a multitude of tools if we are to be faithful artists.

I hope this book has helped you to become a little more proficient with one of those tools. I hope it has helped you to find evocative controlling images for your sermons, images that will effectively propel your sermon themes and accomplish your sermon goals, images that will help you write engaging sermons for a whole new generation of God's people.

Notes

1. The Controlling Image

1. This hard-chair/soft-chair metaphor is attributed to Fred B. Craddock, *Preaching* (Nashville: Abingdon Press, 1985), 84–85, in Michael Graves, *The Fully Alive Preacher: Recovering from Homiletical Burnout* (Philadelphia: Westminster John Knox, 2006), 41–42.

2. Paul Scott Wilson, *The Four Pages of the Sermon: A Guide to Biblical Preaching* (Nashville: Abingdon Press, 1999).

3. Thomas G. Long, *The Witness of Preaching* (Louisville: John Knox Press, 1989).

4. My instinct to choose the "do it all for God's glory" option is rooted in my theological tradition. I come from a stream of the Dutch Reformed tradition influenced by Abraham Kuyper. We tend to see creation as belonging to God, not the devil. We tend to see the kingdom as advancing rather than in retreat. We believe that all human gifts are God glorifying when properly ordered. Our favorite quote from Kuyper is, "There is not a square inch in the whole domain of our human existence over which Christ, who is Sovereign over all, does not cry, 'Mine!'" (Abraham Kuyper, "Sphere Sovereignty (1880)," in *Abraham Kuyper: A Centennial Reader*, ed. James D. Bratt [Grand Rapids: Eerdmans, 1998], 488.)

5. It is worth noting that Paul himself was a formidable practitioner of craft. His considerable rhetorical skill is on display in all his writing, and he used rhetorical forms and strategies (chiasm, for example) in all his letters. See Ralph P. Martin, *New Testament Foundations: A Guide for Christian Students*, vol. 2 (Grand Rapids: Eerdmans, 1978), 241.

6. Paul Scott Wilson, *Broken Words* (Nashville: Abingdon Press, 2004), 23.

7. Sidney Greidanus, *The Modern Preacher and the Ancient Text* (Grand Rapids: Eerdmans, 1988), 131.

8. Bryan Chappell, *Christ-Centered Preaching: Redeeming the Expository Sermon* (Grand Rapids: Baker, 2005), 44.

9. Long, *The Witness of Preaching*, 86.

10. Paul Scott Wilson, *Preaching as Poetry: Beauty, Goodness, and Truth in Every Sermon* (Nashville: Abingdon Press, 2014), 33.

11. Sid Greidanus distinguishes between textual theme and sermon theme. The textual theme is the message that the text had for its original audience/readers. The sermon theme is the message that the text has for the preacher's congregation. This is a valid and helpful distinction and one that must be kept in mind when formulating a theme.

12. Greidanus, *The Modern Preacher*, 138.

13. Long, *The Witness of Preaching*, 87.

14. I've borrowed this language from my preaching colleagues at Calvin Theological Seminary.

15. Wilson, *The Four Pages*, 43.

16. Ibid., 44.

17. The nature of a goal statement will be further fleshed out, but for now, think of a goal statement as a statement of what the preacher wants a sermon to accomplish in the lives of the listeners.

18. Long, *The Witness of Preaching*, 81.

19. Ibid., 80.

20. Greidanus, *The Modern Preacher*, 129.

21. Long, *The Witness of Preaching*, 86, emphasis added.

22. Ibid., 86–87.

23. Virginia Postrel, *The Power of Glamour: Longing and the Art of Visual Persuasion* (New York: Simon and Schuster, 2013), 67–68.

24. James K. A. Smith, *Desiring the Kingdom: Worship, Worldview, and Cultural Formation* (Grand Rapids: Baker Academic, a division of Baker Publishing Group, 2009), 17–18. Used by permission.

25. Ibid., 17n2.

26. Thomas Troeger, *Imagining a Sermon* (Nashville: Abingdon Press, 1990), 26.

27. Paul Scott Wilson, *The Imagination of the Heart* (Nashville: Abingdon Press, 1988), 20.

28. For a summary of this trend, see Lucy Lind Hogan, "Introduction: Poetics and the Context of Preaching," in *The New Interpreter's Handbook of Preaching*, ed. Paul Scott Wilson (Nashville: Abingdon Press, 2008), 173–175.

29. Wilson, *Preaching as Poetry*, xiv.

30. Smith, *Desiring the Kingdom*, 51–53.

31. James K. A. Smith, *Imagining the Kingdom: How Worship Works* (Grand Rapids: Baker Academic, 2013), 162.

32. Ibid.

33. Thomas Troeger concurs: "None of this imaginative work precludes doing careful scholarly work: looking at the passage in its context, finding out what exegetes have to say about the parable, reading it in Greek, Hebrew and various translations, and using all the scholarly tools at one's disposal. Far from being antithetical, scholarship and imagination feed and stimulate each other" ("Imagination/Creativity," in Wilson, *The New Interpreter's Handbook of Preaching*, 190).

34. Barbara Brown Taylor, *The Preaching Life* (Lanham, MD: Cowley, 1993), 82.

35. Ibid., 80, 82.

36. Ibid., 83.

37. Ibid., 80.

38. Ibid.

39. Wilson, *The Imagination of the Heart*, 16.

40. Wilson, *The Four Pages*, 10.

41. Ibid., 10–11.

42. Here's how Wilson puts it: "We may understand [the imagination] as the bringing together of two ideas that might not otherwise be connected and developing the creative energy they generate" (*Imagination of the Heart*, 32). This notion of pairing opposites reflects Coleridge's understanding of how the imagination works.

43. Wilson, *The Four Pages*, 33–57

44. Ibid., 51.

45. Ibid., 50.

2. Controlling Images: A Field Study

1. Paul Scott Wilson, *The Four Pages of the Sermon: A Guide to Biblical Preaching* (Nashville: Abingdon Press, 1999), 51.

2. Barbara Brown Taylor, *The Preaching Life* (Lanham, MD: Cowley, 1993), 154.

3. Ibid.

4. Ibid., 157.

5. Ibid., 158.

6. Ibid.

7. Ibid., 161.

8. James O. Rose, "The Big Valley," in *Biblical Sermons: How Twelve Preachers Apply the Principles of Haddon W. Robinson*, ed. Haddon W. Robinson (Grand Rapids: Baker Books, 1989), 54–55.

9. Throughout this book I use the word "propel" to describe an effective image. It's not a technical term, but when I use it I am describing an image that is evocative and strong in connotative imagery. A propulsive image doesn't close down the imagination of the viewer/listener but sends his or her mind spinning out into other associations and stories.

10. Martin Copenhaver, "Forsaken with Jesus," in *Best Sermons 1*, ed. James Cox (San Francisco: HarperCollins, 1990), 126.

11. Ibid., 127.

12. Ibid., 129.

13. Ibid., 129.

14. What I call a "controlling phrase" Paul Scott Wilson sometimes calls an "acoustical image." It is possible that for some people, musicians perhaps, an acoustical image can be even stronger than a visual one. I once heard a sermon given by my colleague Scott Hoezee in which he symbolized the brevity of life with what might best be described as a controlling sound. When he wanted to communicate the frailty of life he made a noise like a puff of wind: "Whoosh." Just like a controlling image, the sound was used repeatedly in the sermon. It was very effective.

15. Frederick Buechner, *The Magnificent Defeat* (San Francisco: HarperCollins, 1966), 44.

16. Ibid., 44–45.

17. Ibid., 47.

18. Ibid.

19. In fact, I think that most pastors adopt a three-point sermon form when they can't find a really strong controlling image. We know that something else would be more memorable, but if it's a busy week and we don't have the luxury of a couple of hours for creative thinking, we reach for the three points. In that sense three-point sermons are the Hamburger Helper of homiletical forms; you'd like to cook something more interesting but if you don't have the time and there's nothing else in the fridge, so, well, Hamburger Helper it is. It's not the greatest meal, but it's serviceable.

20. Fleming Rutledge, *The Bible and The New York Times* (Grand Rapids: Eerdmans, 1998), 67.

21. Here is the homiletical move Fleming uses to make this controlling idea universal: "'There should have been more to it all.' If you are too young to know this feeling, don't worry, you'll get there." Ibid., 68.

22. Ibid., 69, emphasis added.

23. Walter Brueggemann, *The Threat of Life* (Minneapolis: Fortress, 1996), 24.

24. Ibid., 26–27.

25. And it really is a moment as opposed to a static image. Here is a specific example of the distinction made: The controlling image is visual but not static. Brueggemann invites the listeners to picture a whole dramatic scene and not just one snapshot.

26. Brueggemann, *The Threat of Life*, 27.

27. Ibid., 28–29.

28. Paul Scott Wilson, e-mail message to author, November 10, 2014. The quotations in the e-mail are from Tim Alamenciak and Wendy Gillis, "Lawyer, Nurse, Soldiers Rushed to Aid of Shooting Victim," *The Star* (Toronto), October 23, 2014, http://www.thestar.com/news /canada/2014/10/23/passerby_barbara_winters_ran_to_help_soldier_at_war_memorial.html.

29. Brueggemann, *The Threat of Life*, 28–29.

30. Buechner, *The Magnificent Defeat*, 45.

31. Taylor, *The Preaching Life*, 161.

32. Ibid., 158.

33. Copenhaver, "Forsaken with Jesus," in Cox, *Best Sermons 1*, 129.

34. Ibid., 130.

35. Wilson, *Broken Words*, 73.

3. What Preachers Can Learn from Poets

1. Mary Oliver, *Rules for the Dance: A Handbook for Reading and Writing Metrical Verse* (Boston: Houghton Mifflin, 1998), 70.

2. Robert Frost, "Stopping by Woods on a Snowy Evening," in *The Road Not Taken: A Selection of Robert Frost's Poems* (New York: Holt and Company, 1971), 183.

3. Robert Frost, "Nothing Gold Can Stay," in *The Road Not Taken*, 243.

4. David Citino, ed., *The Eye of the Poet: Six Views of the Art and Craft of Poetry* (New York: Oxford University Press, 2002), 178.

5. Ted Kooser and Steve Cox, *Writing Brave and Free* (Lincoln: Bison Books, 2006), 21.

6. Robert Frost, "The Figure a Poem Makes," in *Modern Poetics*, ed. James Scully (New York: McGraw Hill, 1965), 56.

7. Kooser and Cox, *Writing Brave and Free*, 21.

8. The poem and her description of its writing are found in a web article: Alex Hoyt, "How Poet Laureate Natasha Trethewey Wrote Her Father's 'Elegy,'" *The Atlantic*, August 14, 2012, http://www.theatlantic.com/entertainment/archive/2012/08/how-poet-laureate-natasha -trethewey-wrote-her-fathers-elegy/261126/.

9. Citino, *The Eye of the Poet*, 188.

10. John Ciardi and Miller Williams, *How Does a Poem Mean?* (Boston: Houghton Mifflin, 1975), 239.

11. This is also the tricky part of images with a strong connotative component. Because they are so dependent on context and personal experience, they can cause emotions in the listener that are the opposite of what the preacher intends. Preachers have the best chance to use connotative imagery well when they know the context of the congregation and when they are sensitive to the minority and fringe members of the congregation. If all your images speak the connotative language of the majority, those on the fringe will feel alienated and misunderstood. See chapter 6 for a fuller discussion of this issue.

12. I use the word *delight* to characterize the moment of seeing mostly because that's the word Frost uses. By using this word, I don't mean to suggest that the image that propels you is always cheerful and sunny. Sometimes the image that starts the journey is dark and sobering. Calling it *delight* only means to suggest that there was a moment of light when the image first struck the imagination.

13. This quotation from Ezra Pound originally appeared in his 1918 essay "A Retrospect," which was reprinted in Scully, *Modern Poetics*, 33.

14. Ted Kooser, *The Poetry Home Repair Manual* (Lincoln: Bison Books, 2005), 94.

15. Ibid., 14.

16. Ibid., 15–16.

17. Obituary for Mary A. "Pink" Mullaney, *Journal Sentinel* (Milwaukee, WI), September 4, 2013, http://www.legacy.com/obituaries/jsonline/obituary.aspx?page=lifestory&pid=166788801.

18. Frost, "The Figure a Poem Makes," in Scully, *Modern Poetics*, 56.

19. Pound, "A Retrospect," in Scully, *Modern Poetics*, 32.

20. Robert Lowell, "The Art of Poetry No. 3," interview by Frederick Seidel, *The Paris Review*, no. 25 (Winter–Spring 1961).

21. There are exceptions to this, of course. There is a kind of poetry made of free association where the poet doesn't want you to think there's any kind of message. This kind of work is to poetry what Jackson Pollock's art is to painting. That kind of poetry may have its place, but it's not really useful to this discussion. As I study poets in this book I'll restrict myself to poets like Frost and Oliver and many others who write poems that do intend to say something specific about the nature of life.

4. Learning from Marketers and Visual Artists

1. Quoted in Virginia Postrel, *The Power of Glamour: Longing and the Art of Visual Persuasion* (New York: Simon and Schuster, 2013), 3.

2. Ibid., 3–4.

3. James K. A. Smith, *Desiring the Kingdom: Worship, Worldview, and Cultural Formation* (Grand Rapids: Baker Academic, a division of Baker Publishing Group, 2009), 76. Used by permission.

4. Ibid.

5. Postrel, *The Power of Glamour*, 4.

6. Ibid.

7. Kevin Roberts, interview, *Frontline*, December 15, 2003, http://www.pbs.org/wgbh/pages/frontline/shows/persuaders/interviews/roberts.html.

8. Douglas Atkin, interview, *Frontline*, February 2, 2004, http://www.pbs.org/wgbh/pages/frontline/shows/persuaders/interviews/atkin.html.

9. Quoted in Postrel, *The Power of Glamour*, 182.

10. Ibid., 141.

11. Obviously for a whole generation of Republicans, the Obama image represents something very different, but the image is iconic regardless of your political allegiance. For both Republicans and Democrats, it's a picture that has that iconic power of projection. It projects a story. For some that story and the emotions associated with it are positive; for others the story is negative.

This brings back the concerns raised in the previous chapter. A connotative image (and images that put people in a story are all richly connotative) is context specific and hard to control. When choosing story-shaped images, preachers should be careful that the story suggested by these images is not always told in terms of the majority. Sometimes the images should evoke the stories of people on the margins. Sensitivity to these issues keeps the eyes of God's people raised above their own concerns and makes sure our angle of vision is as wide as God's kingdom.

12. I've often heard this phenomenon referenced by people who warn against using stories that are "too good." I think that's probably wrongheaded. When a story distracts from the text of the sermon and renders a listener unable to recall the theme, it's probably because the story pointed away from the text and the theme instead of toward it. It's a sign that theme and image were not properly aligned (see chapter 1). When a really good story points at the text and the theme, it makes the biblical material *more* memorable, not less.

13. Postrel, *The Power of Glamour*, 20.

14. Smith, *Desiring the Kingdom*, 53.

15. I was first alerted to the difference between these two pictures in Postrel, *The Power of Glamour*, 87.

16. Chip Heath and Dan Heath, *Made to Stick* (New York: Random House, 2007), 166.

17. Ibid.

18. Frederick Buechner, *The Magnificent Defeat* (New York: Seabury, 1966), 18.

5. How to Find a Controlling Image

1. David Citino, ed., *The Eye of the Poet: Six Views of the Art and Craft of Poetry* (New York: Oxford University Press, 2002), 178.

2. Barbara Brown Taylor, *The Preaching Life* (Lanham, MD: Cowley, 1993), 80.

3. Referenced in Annie Dillard, *The Writing Life* (New York: Harper and Row, 1989), 75.

4. It seems to me that when we read devotionally we are consciously trying to approach a text from the angle of heart and imagination rather than the angle of analysis. When we're reading devotionally we ask, "What is the Spirit saying to me and my life and my world through this text?" When we read more analytically we say, "I want to understand what this text means." When we read devotionally we are looking for a personal word. When we read analytically we are looking to understand the text in its original context. Intellect and imagination are involved in both kinds of readings, but the intellect is primary in the analysis, while the imagination takes the lead in the devotion.

5. Gabriel O'Donnell, "Reading for Holiness: *Lectio Divina*," in *Spiritual Traditions for the Contemporary Church*. eds. Gabriel O'Donnell and Robin Maas (Nashville: Abingdon Press, 1990), 50.

6. Luke Dysinger, "How to Practice Lectio Divina," Beliefnet, http://www.beliefnet.com/Faiths/Catholic/2000/08/How-To-Practice-Lectio-Divina.aspx.

7. Michael J. Quicke, *360-Degree Preaching* (Grand Rapids: Baker Academic, 2003), 143.

8. James C. Wilhoit and Evan B. Howard, *Discovering* Lectio Divina (Downers Grove, IL: InterVarsity, 2012), 79.

9. Ibid., 63–64.

10. Ibid.

11. Ibid.

12. Ibid.

13. Ibid.

14. Robert Frost, "The Figure a Poem Makes," in *Modern Poetics*, ed. James Scully (New York: McGraw Hill, 1965), 57.

15. Ted Kooser, *The Poetry Home Repair Manual* (Lincoln, NE: Bison Books, 2005), 93.

16. Ted Kooser, "Cosmetics Department," in ibid., 99.

17. This exercise is similar to one suggested by Paul Scott Wilson in *The Practice of Preaching* (Nashville: Abingdon Press, 2007), 60, but in his exercise Wilson has students list the concerns of the text rather than the images. He defines the concerns as "any thought, idea, or emotion expressed by a biblical text."

18. Ted Kooser and Steve Cox, *Writing Brave and Free* (Lincoln, NE: Bison Books, 2006), 21.

19. Ibid.

20. Roger Mitchell, "Tell By Showing," in *The Practice of Poetry*, ed. Robin Behn and Chris Twichell (New York: HarperCollins, 1992), 56.

21. No one, that is, except maybe people like James Joyce (or Jackson Pollock in the world of painting)—and even they are using their art to make a point about art. They are still telling something.

22. Mitchell, "Tell By Showing," in Behn and Twichell, *The Practice of Poetry*, 57–58.

23. Ibid.

24. Carol Muske, "Translations: Idea to Image (for a group)," in Behn and Twichell, *The Practice of Poetry*, 8.

25. Sid Greidanus distinguishes between textual theme and sermon theme. The textual theme is the message that the text had for its original audience/readers. The sermon theme is the message that the text has for the preacher's congregation. This is a valid and helpful distinction and one that must be kept in mind when formulating a theme. See Sidney Greidanus, *The Modern Preacher and the Ancient Text* (Grand Rapids: Eerdmans, 1988), 138.

26. Ibid.

27. Kooser and Cox, *Writing Brave and Free*, 57.

28. Ibid., 57.

29. Tim Ladwig, *Psalm Twenty-Three* (Grand Rapids: Eerdmans, 1997).

6. Sermons and Image on Screens

1. Robert Gaskins, "Viewpoint: How PowerPoint Changed Microsoft and My Life," BBC News, July 30, 2012, http://www.bbc.com/news/technology-19042236.

2. Screens are a very Protestant phenomenon. They are far less prevalent in Catholic churches and they are virtually nonexistent in Eastern Orthodox churches.

3. Marc T. Newman, "Video Clips," in *The New Interpreter's Handbook of Preaching*, ed. Paul Scott Wilson (Nashville: Abingdon Press, 2008), 209.

4. Paul Wilson, *Preaching as Poetry* (Nashville: Abingdon Press, 2014), xiv.

5. Ibid.

6. For example, Len Wilson and Jason Moore, *The Wired Church 2.0* (Nashville: Abingdon Press, 2008).

7. See Paul Scott Wilson, "New Homiletic," in Wilson, *The New Interpreter's Handbook of Preaching*, 398.

8. Elizabeth Bumiller, "We Have Met the Enemy and He Is PowerPoint," *New York Times*, April 26, 2010.

9. Garr Reynolds, *Presentation Zen* (Berkeley: New Riders, 2012), 134.

10. Wilson and Moore, *The Wired Church 2.0*, 52, 60.

11. Guy Kawasaki, "The 10/20/30 Rule of PowerPoint," *How to Change the World* (blog), December 30, 2005, http://blog.guykawasaki.com/2005/12/the_102030_rule.html.

12. Reynolds, *Presentation Zen*, 66.

13. Ibid.

14. My colleague Scott Hoezee has an additional concern about using the slide to do all the heavy lifting of communication. If the preacher relies too much on the text and images of his PowerPoint presentations, he or she may lose some of the verbal powers of description that every preacher needs. Every preacher needs to be able to paint a picture with words; screens cannot become a substitute for this ability.

15. Kenton Anderson, "Best PowerPoint Practices for Preaching," *Preaching.org* (blog), March 6, 2014, http://www.preaching.org/bestpowerpointpractices/.

16. Troy McQueen, "Visually Enhanced Technology," *Adventist Messenger*, November 15, 2009.

17. Anderson, "Best PowerPoint Presentations."

18. Steve Koster, "Four Ways to Use a Slide: Illustration," *Leading with Light* (blog), March 15, 2005, http://www.leadingwithlight.com/2005/03/four_ways_to_us.html#more.

19. Frederica Mathewes-Green, *The Open Door: Entering the Sanctuary of Icons and Prayer* (Brewster, MA: Paraclete, 2003), 14–15.

20. Ibid., 15.

21. Ibid., 24. This description of a "deeper down" place that comes before the regions of thought and emotion sounds strikingly similar to Jamie Smith's descriptions of how the imagination precedes reason in our construal of the word.

22. Quoted in Reynolds, *Presentation Zen*, 91.

23. Quoted in ibid., 21.

24. This image does not reproduce well in black and white so I was unable to share it in this book. It is readily viewable online.

25. Carl Sagan, *Pale Blue Dot: A Vision of the Human Future in Space* (New York: Random House, 1997), 6–7.

26. Eileen Crowley, *Liturgical Art for a Media Culture* (Collegeville, MN: Liturgical Press, 2007), 70.

27. Eileen Crowley, "Media Art in Worship: The Potential for a New Liturgical Art, Its Pastoral and Theological Challenges" (plenary address for the Institute for Liturgical Studies, Valparaiso, IN, April 20, 2004). See also her chapter "A Model for Liturgical Media Ministry: Communal Co-Creation," in Crowley, *Liturgical Art for a Media Culture*.

28. Marc Nelesen and Darrin Sculley, "Using Screens in Worship: One Church's Criteria," *Reformed Worship* 72 (June 2004): 42-43. Emphasis added.

29. Scott Hoezee, *Actuality: Stories of Real Life for Sermons That Matter* (Nashville: Abingdon Press, 2014), 45–46.

30. Elizabeth Steele Halstead, Paul Detterman, Joyce Borger, and John D. Witvliet, *Dwelling with Philippians* (Grand Rapids: Eerdmans, 2010).

31. Marc Newman, "Video Clips," in Wilson, *The New Interpreter's Handbook of Preaching*, 210.

32. Virginia Postrel, *The Power of Glamour: Longing and the Art of Visual Persuasion* (New York: Simon and Schuster, 2013), 177.

33. Crowley, "Media Art in Worship."

Bibliography

Anderson, Kenton. "Best PowerPoint Practices for Preaching." *Preaching.org* (blog). March 6, 2014. http://www.preaching.org/bestpowerpointpractices/.

Brueggemann, Walter. *The Threat of Life*. Minneapolis, Fortress: 1996.

Buechner, Frederick. *The Magnificent Defeat*. San Francisco: HarperCollins, 1966.

Bumiller, Elizabeth. "We Have Met the Enemy and He Is PowerPoint," *New York Times*, April 26, 2010.

Chappell, Bryan. *Christ-Centered Preaching: Redeeming the Expository Sermon*. Grand Rapids: Baker, 2005.

Ciardi, John, and Miller Williams. *How Does a Poem Mean?* Boston: Houghton Mifflin, 1975.

Citino, David, ed. *The Eye of the Poet: Six Views of the Art and Craft of Poetry*. New York: Oxford University Press, 2002.

Copenhaver, Martin. "Forsaken with Jesus." In *Best Sermons 1*. Edited by James Cox. San Francisco: HarperCollins, 1990.

Crowley, Ellen. *Liturgical Art for a Media Culture*. Collegeville, MN: Liturgical Press, 2007.

———. "Media Art in Worship: The Potential for a New Liturgical Art, Its Pastoral and Theological Challenges." Plenary address for the Institute for Liturgical Studies, Valparaiso, IN, April 20, 2004.

Dillard, Annie. *The Writing Life*. New York: Harper and Row, 1989.

Dysinger, Luke. "How to Practice Lectio Divina." Beliefnet. http://www.beliefnet.com/Faiths/Catholic/2000/08/How-To-Practice-Lectio-Divina.aspx.

Frost, Robert. "The Figure a Poem Makes." In *Modern Poetics*. Edited by James Scully. New York, McGraw Hill, 1965.

———. "Nothing Gold Can Stay." In *The Road Not Taken: A Selection of Robert Frost's Poems*. New York: Holt and Company, 1971.

———. "Stopping by Woods on a Snowy Evening." In *The Road Not Taken: A Selection of Robert Frost's Poems*. New York: Holt and Company, 1971.

Gaskins, Robert. "Viewpoint: How PointPoint Changed Microsoft and My Life." *BBC News.* July 30, 2012. http://www.bbc.com/news/technology-19042236.

Graves, Michael. *The Fully Alive Preacher.* Philadelphia: Westminster John Knox, 2006.

Greidanus, Sidney. *The Modern Preacher and the Ancient Text.* Grand Rapids: Eerdmans, 1988.

Halstead, Elizabeth Steele, Paul Detterman, Joyce Borger, and John D. Witvliet. *Dwelling with Philippians.* Grand Rapids: Eerdmans, 2010.

Heath, Chip, and Dan Heath. *Made to Stick.* New York: Random House, 2007.

Hoezee, Scott. *Actuality: Real Life Stories for Sermons That Matter.* Nashville: Abingdon Press, 2014.

Hogan, Lucy Lind. "Introduction: Poetics and the Context of Preaching." In *The New Interpreter's Handbook of Preaching.* Edited by Paul Scott Wilson. Nashville: Abingdon Press, 2008.

Hoyt, Alex. "How Poet Laureate Natasha Trethewey Wrote Her Father's 'Elegy.'" *The Atlantic.* August 14, 2012. http://www.theatlantic.com/entertainment/archive/2012/08/how-poet-laureate-natasha-trethewey-wrote-her-fathers-elegy/261126/.

Kawasaki, Guy. "The 10/20/30 Rule of PowerPoint." *How to Change the World* (blog). December 30, 2005. http://blog.guykawasaki.com/2005/12/the_102030_rule.html.

Kooser, Ted. *The Poetry Home Repair Manual.* Lincoln, NE: Bison Books, 2005.

Kooser, Ted, and Steve Cox. *Writing Brave and Free.* Lincoln, NE: Bison Books, 2006.

Koster, Steve. "Four Ways to Use a Slide: Illustration." *Leading with Light* (blog). March 15, 2005. http://www.leadingwithlight.com/2005/03/four_ways_to_us.html#more.

Kuyper, Abraham. "Sphere Sovereignty (1880)." In *Abraham Kuyper: A Centennial Reader.* Edited by James D. Bratt. Grand Rapids: Eerdmans, 1998.

Ladwig, Tim. *Psalm Twenty-Three.* Grand Rapids: Eerdmans, 1997.

Long, Thomas G. *The Witness of Preaching.* Louisville: John Knox Press, 1989.

Lowell, Robert. "The Art of Poetry No. 3." Interview by Frederick Seidel. *The Paris Review,* no. 25 (Winter–Spring 1961).

Martin, Ralph P. *New Testament Foundations: A Guide for Christian Students.* Vol. 2, *The Acts, the Letters, the Apocalypse.* Grand Rapids: Eerdmans, 1978.

Mathewes-Green, Frederica. *The Open Door: Entering the Sanctuary of Icons and Prayer.* Brewster, MA: Paraclete, 2003.

Mitchell, Roger. "Tell By Showing." In *The Practice of Poetry*. Edited by Robin Behn and Chris Twichell. New York: HarperCollins, 1992.

Muske, Carol. "Translations: Idea to Image." In *The Practice of Poetry*. Edited by Robin Behn and Chris Twichell. New York: HarperCollins, 1992.

Nelesen, Marc, and Darrin Sculley. "Using Screens in Worship: One Church's Criteria." *Reformed Worship* 72, (June 2004): 42-43.

Newman, Marc T. "Video Clips." In *The New Interpreter's Handbook of Preaching*. Edited by Paul Scott Wilson. Nashville: Abingdon Press, 2008.

Obituary for Mary A. "Pink" Mullaney. *Journal Sentinel* (Milwaukee, WI). September 4, 2013. http://www.legacy.com/obituaries/jsonline/obituary.aspx?page =lifestory&pid=166788801.

O'Donnell, Gabriel. "Reading for Holiness: *Lectio Divina*." In *Spiritual Traditions for the Contemporary Church*. Edited by Gabriel O'Donnell and Robin Maas. Nashville: Abingdon Press, 1990.

Oliver, Mary. *Rules for the Dance: A Handbook for Reading and Writing Metrical Verse*. Boston: Houghton Mifflin, 1998.

Postrel, Virginia. *The Power of Glamour: Longing and the Art of Visual Persuasion*. New York: Simon and Schuster, 2013.

Pound, Ezra. "A Retrospect." In *Modern Poetics*. Edited by James Scully. New York: McGraw-Hill, 1965.

Quicke, Michael J. *360-Degree Preaching*. Grand Rapids: Baker Academic, 2003.

Reynolds, Garr. *Presentation Zen*. Berkeley: New Riders, 2012.

Rose, James O. "The Big Valley." In *Biblical Sermons: How Twelve Preachers Apply the Principles of Haddon W. Robinson*. Edited by Haddon W. Robinson. Grand Rapids: Baker Books, 1989).

Rutledge, Fleming. *The Bible and* The New York Times. Grand Rapids: Eerdmans, 1998.

Sagan, Carl. *Pale Blue Dot: A Vision of the Human Future in Space*. New York: Random House, 1997.

Smith, James K. A. *Desiring the Kingdom: Worship, Worldview, and Cultural Formation*. Grand Rapids: Baker Academic, a division of Baker Publishing Group, 2009. Used by permission.

———. *Imagining the Kingdom: How Worship Works*. Grand Rapids: Baker Academic, 2013.

Taylor, Barbara Brown. *The Preaching Life*. Lanham, MD: Cowley, 1993.

Troeger, Thomas. "Imagination/Creativity." In *The New Interpreter's Handbook of Preaching*. Edited by Paul Scott Wilson. Nashville: Abingdon Press, 2008.

———. *Imagining a Sermon*. Nashville: Abingdon Press, 1990.

Wilhoit, James C., and Evan B. Howard. *Discovering* Lectio Divina. Downers Grove, IL: InterVarsity, 2012.

Wilson, Len, and Jason Moore. *The Wired Church 2.0.* Nashville: Abingdon Press, 2008.

Wilson, Paul Scott. *Broken Words: Reflections on the Craft of Preaching.* Nashville: Abingdon Press, 2004.

———. *The Four Pages of the Sermon: A Guide to Biblical Preaching.* Nashville: Abingdon Press, 1999.

———. *Imagination of the Heart.* Nashville: Abingdon Press, 1988.

———. "New Homiletic." In *The New Interpreter's Handbook of Preaching.* Edited by Paul Scott Wilson. Nashville: Abingdon Press, 2008.

———. *Preaching as Poetry: Beauty, Goodness, and Truth in Every Sermon.* Nashville: Abingdon Press, 2014.

———. *The Practice of Preaching.* Nashville: Abingdon Press, 2007.